GOD
CREATION
AND THE
HOLOGRAPHIC
UNIVERSE

Tip McPartland

God, Creation and the Holographic Universe

By Tip McPartland

Cover art image courtesy of D. Nelson / Illustris Collaboration
Cover design and interior layout by Karen McPartland

ISBN: 9798323625130

Printed in the United States of America

Amazon Publishing
4900 Lacross Rd
North Charleston, SC 29406-6558

Table of Contents

PREFACE 1

1: SCIENCE, CREATION AND OUR PURPOSE IN LIFE 8

2: BEYOND $E=mc^2$ TO THE GREAT CYCLE OF CREATION 21

3: THE HOLOGRAPHIC UNIVERSE, THE AKASHIC RECORD AND GOD 30

4: THE HOLOGRAPHIC PRINCIPLE IN EVERYDAY LIFE 41

5: DARK MATTER VERSUS DARK ENERGY: WHAT IS DARK MATTER? 51

6: DEATH: THE END OF THE ILLUSION OF SEPARATENESS .55

7: NEW SCIENCE FROM OUR OLDEST FAITH 66

8: THE SEVEN CENTERS OF CONSCIOUSNESS 69

9: THE ARCHITECTURE OF THE SPIRIT 103

10: GUIDED EVOLUTION AND THE LEVELS OF CONSCIOUSNESS 110

11: WHY DOES GOD LET BAD THINGS HAPPEN? 132

12: HOW RELIGIONS WORK AND HOW THEY CAN WORK TOGETHER 143

13: WHAT'S BEHIND THE WORLD'S SIX GREAT FAITHS 157

14: HOW TO PREVENT FUTURE WARS 185

PREFACE

This book is here to refocus the eyes of science and religion so that they take on a binocular vision that gives full dimension to the truth about *who* we are, *what* we are, *why* we are, and most incredibly, *where* we are – a holographic universe created by God.

It will splay out for all to see the incredible and profound implications scientists have failed to see in their own recent cosmological breakthroughs, and by doing so, at last decode the confusing jumble that remains to us from ancient spiritual knowledge.

In the first few chapters it digs deeply into the reality-shattering implications of the holographic universe and quantum entanglement, showing us how our daily lives are not just impacted, *but shaped*, by these supposedly abstract and esoteric concepts. In fact, we will demonstrate that quantum entanglement colors virtually everything we do from falling in love to playing tennis.

Further in we explore the spiritual aspects of this new science in the context of the major religions, offering up fresh and credible answers to many of life's most important questions. Does God exist and how can we find Him, or Her, or It? Is there life after death, and if so, what is its nature? Did God create the universe, and if so, how? What is the answer to the conflict over evolution and intelligent design? What is the surprising but simple truth about our actual purpose in life?

This book also explains the amazingly simple way that all religions actually work, and makes it clear why and how just about any faith can produce an authentic religious experience — whether that faith is "true" or not. This explanation of how and why any and all religions work can help "true believers" to understand each other's faiths. This can pave the way for greater harmony between religions and may help to ease the religious conflicts that pose an existential threat to our world in our time.

It's becoming clear that the recent breakthrough discoveries in astronomy and physics are coming very close to answering the great riddles of the universe. It is time to lay some key girders into the bridge being built between science and religion, but the problem is that these two spheres have their own mindsets and vernaculars. But unlike the other volumes that attempt to build this bridge, this book is not written by a Ph.D., usually a physicist or mathematician, who cannot help using academic jargon and developing complex and technical arguments that are meaningful primarily to fellow scientists. In fact, these scholarly writers have to write with an eye to defending their academic flank, lest they be regarded as less than rigorous by their peers, so they are in a way boxed in and must use overly complicated language. This writer has the greatest respect for the pioneering work, compelling ideas, and deeply thorough presentations of Paul Davies, Ervin László, Leonard Susskind and Amit Goswami to name a few, and there is no intent to challenge their excellent writings, just to make it clear that this book has different goals, simpler presentations and broader content, while perhaps reaching even more profound conclusions. It is also worth giving a nod to journalist Lynn McTaggert whose work may be more accessible to a popular sensibility than the others.

We are living in a time when there is a well-spring of new ideas, and new ideas are at the heart of this book, some built over a foundation of reading and research, but some that seem to come from the subconscious or even deeper — realizations and perhaps even revelations. Nonetheless, anyone who reads and enjoys this book would be well advised to visit the work of all these excellent and important authors, as well as others who are helping to establish the integration of the scientific with the spiritual as an exciting and important new genre in non-fiction literature.

Lay readers who enjoy this genre of book will be pleased to find that these new concepts, as well as new explanations of material included in other cutting-edge books, are presented very simply and in plain English here as is appropriate for their sensibility. However, not only is none of the really crucial information omitted, only reduced are the mountains of supporting detail and theoretical underpinnings. However, many of the extremely important corollaries and conclusions reached here follow directly from the material presented in other volumes, yet many of these next-generation ideas are sadly not to be found there.

In short, this book finally answers many of the questions raised in the work of Davies, McTaggert and the others mentioned earlier who have seen the potential and possibilities created by recent discoveries to build that badly needed bridge between our spiritual/religious traditions and today's bleeding-edge science. This potential has been evident since some thinkers have extrapolated the mind-boggling implications of the Holographic Principle discovered and explored by Alain Aspect, Charles Thorn, Gerard 't Hooft, David Bohm and Leonard Susskind. This book finally realizes that potential with breakthrough concepts that are intuitive and obvious to the reader once read. They are also easily understood as well because of the simple, jargon-free language.

The lack of jargon extends beyond the simplification of scientific ideas into the manner that certain spiritual concepts are presented, in this case avoiding much of the confusing Sanskrit verbiage found in most other explanations of esoteric spiritual and religious materials. Not only are these Sanskrit terms and names hard to read, difficult to pronounce and impossible to remember, they are in any event meaningless to most Western readers and irrelevant to understanding the underlying concepts. But sometimes a chakra is just a chakra, and that word is now part of the English language.

Although useful, informative and hopefully engaging for just about anyone, this book may be particularly valuable for three groups of people who, taken together, include broad segments of the adult population throughout the world.

One of these three groups might be called the "rational skeptics" who find it hard to believe in God because their secular humanism or scientific outlook precludes belief in *any* religion's "supernatural" cosmology and various other "mythologies." These people often react to what they consider unbelievable stories in the Bible or other scriptures by concluding that religions are nothing but fiction and fable, and many react by becoming agnostics or atheists. They need an understanding of God and religion that doesn't violate their intellectual standards, and they can find it here.

Another group comprises "true believers" in any of the world's great faiths, or even those not so great, who see little truth in the others. Ironically, they probably regard the other faiths much as the "rational skeptics" regard theirs. There is much here to benefit them, as well as the world they influence, and jeopardize, so much.

The third group is people who have religious leanings, but also religious doubts. They're not satisfied with the answers and information they've received from the traditional religions and have perhaps explored alternative beliefs or spiritual systems. They are busy living their lives and are not on religious quests, but they nonetheless would like to find better answers to their spiritual questions.

For the true believers, this book can open doors to real understanding of why billions of sincere and devout people believe in other religions besides theirs, and why the experiences these other religions give their adherents are genuine. The true believer should hopefully come to understand why and how these other religions can bring people together with God, and, much more important, *that they do* in fact bring people into touch with the Divine.

The rational skeptics, who are usually highly-intelligent, independent thinkers that regard traditional religions as supernatural myths and dysfunctional emotional crutches, "the opiate of the people" will learn to separate the wheat from the chaff. They need to learn how to sidestep their disbelief in their traditional religion's creation narrative, cosmology and supernatural stories and instead focus on the benefits they *can* gain from their religion's highly-effective core modality. With that knowledge, and with the right understanding of what their traditional religion's true functionality is, and how it works, even highly-demanding rational skeptics can have fulfilling religious experiences through their traditional religions' practices. And they can receive this benefit in spite of continuing to intellectually reject many, *or even all*, of its "mythologies" and doctrines.

Those many people in the middle who are not committed believers or extreme skeptics, but who have the desire to find religious beliefs in spite of their religious doubts, can benefit from this book. It can offer an understanding of God, religion and the universe that may ring true to them and does not conflict with their common sense and whatever level of scientific knowledge they may have. They need an approach to religion that encompasses a credible, rational, yet still inspiring, understanding of God and His (or Her or Its) relationship to them. They may also seek better answers to the universal riddles, answers in which they can believe, without pretending, compromising or making uncomfortable leaps of faith. This book will provide credible ideas that will help these readers to sort out their thoughts.

There is nothing in this book that will challenge or attempt to invalidate any articles of faith for true believers, or for those who are religious but less committed – it is emphatically not about challenging anyone's traditional or adopted religion. However, there is information here that will help them to open their minds to the validity of other peoples' faiths, at least for those who believe in them, for example a Christian hopefully coming to respect the sincerity of a devout Muslim's beliefs and even the efficacy of his practices.

While taking an eclectic approach to the world's religions, this book will not try to tell you, as Huston Smith does, that all religions are the same – they are not. It will not try to tell you, as Stephen Prothero does, that different religions worship different Gods – they don't. There can only be one Creator of the universe, no matter what He, She or It is called.

Now, in our first chapters let's delve into the implications of the holographic universe, quantum entanglement, and other breakthrough science. Then we'll see how it's possible that a rainbow of different religions with completely different modalities and pathways, can all help people to find the one God.

1: SCIENCE, CREATION AND OUR PURPOSE IN LIFE

Our relationship with God should not be about what we get, but about what we give. Ultimately, the most important aspect of religious practice is serving God. It is interesting that our function on this planet gives an almost literal meaning to this phrase, because we are actually on this planet to "feed" something to God. To understand what this means and how it can be, we must go back to the beginning, and understand how God made the universe and what He made it from.

The creation story we'll be presenting later in more detail is scientifically grounded while encompassing and respecting traditional beliefs. In fact, it is in line with many religious thinkers' immediate reactions on hearing of the Big Bang theory. When this theory was first promulgated by scientists, these religious thinkers pointed to the Big Bang as scientific recognition that there was a singular act of creation, and thus, a Creator.

In January of 2011, His Holiness Pope Benedict XVI announced that he believed that God was the cause of the Big Bang. However one may feel about papal infallibility, in this instance the Pope appears to be correct.

Not surprisingly, scientists have developed various theories to explain how the Big Bang could occur without the instrumentality of God. They believe that there could be a first action without a first cause, but there is no solid scientific evidence for any such thing. Not only that, but the physicists' consensus theory about the cause of the Big Bang leads to contradictions that they have not yet been able to resolve, and which scientists freely acknowledge do self-invalidate their theories.

Physicists believe that the Big Bang occurred spontaneously due to instabilities in what they call the "quantum vacuum." This is a zero-sum scenario because according to this theory, all the matter in the universe arose essentially from "nothing" and thus could be folded back into, well, nothing. But for this zero-sum scenario to be true, all the matter in the universe created in the Big Bang would have to be balanced by an equal amount of anti-matter. This would have to occur because the sum of the matter and anti-matter would have to cancel out to zero, and thus theoretically the universe could be spun out of nothing and returned to nothing. However, there are two severe problems with this zero-sum theory. First, there is no equal amount of anti-matter in evidence. In fact, there is basically none, let alone enough to achieve parity with the matter. This rather severe contradiction is known as a "CP violation" with C meaning "charge conjugation" and P meaning "parity inversion" which means in simple

English, "Where is the anti-matter that must be here if our theory is correct?" Furthermore, if there was anti-matter created in the zero-sum scenario, it would have immediately annihilated all the matter (and vice versa) resulting in an empty universe, or at least one with no matter, but there would have been a release of an enormous amount of energy, in fact there is nothing currently known by physics that releases more energy. So, you would not get "nothing" even in this scenario. Hence, the zero-sum idea is false on its face.

But it is possible that anti-matter has repulsive instead of attractive gravity. Work in the exotic field of electrogravitics, beyond the scope of this book, have raised this as a distinct possibility. If this were so, the anti-matter might have been driven by its own mutual repulsion to an area far beyond our universe of conventional matter, perhaps existing to this day as a distant ring far outside all of the universe's conventional matter. But even if this were so, were matter and anti-matter to somehow come together and annihilate each other, the release of energy would be well beyond enormous, and the release and existence of this energy would still solidly contradict the zero-sum theory, because that energy would have had to come into the system from somewhere to trigger the creation of matter and anti-matter from the quantum vacuum.

The zero-sum theory that matter arose spontaneously from the quantum vacuum in the Big Bang is actually a non-starter, with no less than two fatal contradictions evident. It appears that the scientists are wrong about their random zero-sum game, but does that mean that the religious thinkers are completely correct about the Big Bang being an act of creation?

The religious thinkers such as Pope Benedict believe that the first action (the Big Bang) did have a first cause, and this cause could only come from the one thing that predated creation, and that of course is the Creator. So then picture God and the void. If the zero-sum scenario is impossible, God must have had something other than the quantum vacuum with which to form all of the universe's matter and energy. Simply put, God needed some major ingredients if He, She or It was to cook up an almost infinite universe. But before matter and energy were created in the Big Bang, there was nothing, no ingredients to stir together into our super massive universe. So, if there was nothing, what did God use? Well, there was something, there was God Himself, Herself or Itself, and in fact that is all there was, and all that was needed.

The only possible explanation is that God created the universe out of His own substance, making the ultimate choice to explosively convert His, Her or Its own pure consciousness into matter and energy at the instant of the Big Bang. Why did He (for simplicity the male pronoun will be used henceforth, but hopefully by now it's clear that this author regards God as beyond gender) make the universe out of Himself, out of His own stuff? The short answer, as we have discussed, is that He had nothing else to work with — before creation, there was only The Creator. If He was to make a universe, and evidently, He was, He had to turn His own pure consciousness into matter and energy.

The great yogi Swami Muktananda, teacher of famous Indians such as Indira Gandhi, came to a similar conclusion from his own spiritual experiences. In his book "I Have Become Alive" he expresses this reality very well:

> God is with all of us, but to understand this we have to understand the structure of the universe. This entire world came into manifestation because of the explosion of the bliss of God. It lives in God's bliss and finally merges into Him. All the forms in the universe are made of nothing but that bliss. The different activities of the world, its infinite and amazing modifications, its various names, its strange and diverse forms, its fascinating and remarkable arts, and its highly refined skills are all the joyful creation of the actor of the universe. Just as a spider spins a web out of its own body, God's Shakti, His own independent and inseparable power, created this universe out of its own being, manifesting it upon its own screen, in total freedom. It did not require any external material to create the universe because it had everything it needed within itself. [1]

With the understanding that God made matter and energy out of His own consciousness, there is no need for a zero-sum mechanism, thus eliminating the CP violation.

There is only the breathtaking realization that consciousness is interchangeable with matter and energy just as they are interchangeable with each other. $E=mc^2$ *needs one more term to denote the equivalence between not just matter and energy, but also consciousness!*

Thus, our cosmos did not have to spring spontaneously out of the void through bizarre quantum shenanigans, any more than frogs grow spontaneously out of mud or flies spring from decaying meat as scientists once thought.

Later, we will expand on this approach to the sequence of events that followed the Big Bang when we reconcile creationist, Darwinist and post-Darwinist thought through a fresh and credible approach to the idea of guided evolution.

God did create life on Earth including us, and as we will see later, the mode of creation He used and that we will present, does not contradict the fossil record, unlike conventional creationism. Interestingly, God's mode of creating the universe bears on His purpose for us, and in fact for all life. Now, in order to make the most of our relationship with God we must also learn what this purpose is and how to best fulfill it.

To begin to understand that purpose, we should explore the ramifications that followed God converting almost infinite amounts of His own consciousness into matter and energy in the Big Bang. One ramification is that like many things in our world, this outpouring of God's energy is part of a cycle. Much like rain falls, flows through our rivers and into our oceans and lakes, and then evaporates back up to the sky to form clouds and again fall as rain, consciousness comes from God and then returns to Him. So, if this is another of the Universe's cycles, starting with God giving of His own consciousness, like water falling as rain, the universe must have a way for that consciousness to return back to Him like water evaporating back up to the clouds. This cycle of consciousness is the most fundamental of all of nature's cycles.

During the last century we learned the truth of Einstein's equation $E=mc^2$, in which matter and energy were shown to be interchangeable. But matter and energy are not the only things in our universe; quantum theory has demonstrated that consciousness — physicists sometimes use the term an "observer" — is also a fundamental element of physics, and by extension, of the universe. As many scientists are starting to discern, consciousness is not an accident of evolution, it is the most fundamental quality there is, rendering even matter and energy as secondary forms. In fact, matter and energy are *not just interchangeable with each other*, but with the third primary quality of the universe (perhaps we should call it the first) which is consciousness. While consciousness is nothing more or less than God's own essence, predating creation as well as driving the Big Bang, it obviously also exists within each of us, and is in fact the only thing we experience directly, all else coming from our senses.

It can be emphatically stated that the true function of all life is to generate, concentrate and refine consciousness and return it to God, to help complete the Great Cycle of Creation that began when God converted His own consciousness to matter and energy in the Big Bang. Thus, among all our own wondrous qualities, we are at our core amazing devices that can turn food, water and air into consciousness and then return it to God for His on-going edification.

But consciousness, like all other non-material essences, exists in various quantum states, or quasi-energetic levels, so our purpose and duty as sentient beings is not just to return some generic form of consciousness to God, but to elevate our consciousness to the highest and most refined level that we can. This is so that as we return our consciousness to God, it is the finest and fullest possible gift, restoring back to Him throughout our lives and in our deaths as much as possible of what He gave to us all in the creation. Later we will learn how to maximize this process, thus truly pleasing God.

A corollary of this understanding of creation, and the sacrifice of much of Himself that God made to drive it, is that we can reinforce our faith, whatever our religion may be, by learning not to blame God for the world's problems, and especially not for our own. As we suggested earlier, in the Big Bang, God expended almost His entire being to create our nearly infinite universe. That is why on the seventh day, as the Judeo-Christian scriptures say, He rested. Please, Judeo-Christians, believe your own scriptures, it does not say "then He paused," it says He *"rested"* and nobody rests unless they've expended a great deal of their energy. He had given the job of creation just about everything He had. Why would He give less? Now, He is still, in a sense, resting from this task, or at least seems to have little inclination to actively micromanage every little corner of His vast creation!

All of the above material may seem speculative, but if it is, it gets less so on an almost daily basis. Science has recently found evidence of the Great Cycle of Creation in their astrophysical equations. This is because they've found what may be God's essence, perhaps the same energy that drove creation, as a force in the universe. While this force itself is not yet detectable, it does have a detectable effect that now appears to sustain the universe and prevent its destruction. They have also proven that this invisible but powerful energy is increasing, and this is as would be predicted if that energy is related to God's continually absorbing consciousness from all of the universe's life in the Great Cycle of Creation scenario. In short, life is the process by which matter and energy are converted back into consciousness and returned to God.

Although many scientists wrongly call this very evident form of God's essence "Dark Energy," this phrase is a misnomer. It is a misnomer *not just* because this newly-discovered constituent of the universe is not "dark," but also because it is *not* energy in the conventional sense. Some scientists further designate it as either "the cosmological constant" which as the name states, is unchanging, while others refer to it as "Quintessence." In the Quintessence model, the strength of the Dark Energy is variable, changing from time to time with causalities that are totally unfathomable to scientists. But perhaps the reason is that Dark Energy is linked to consciousness, and thus to God, and the changes in it are willful, and, as observed, sustaining and necessary to the universe's continuing existence.

Dark Energy is the term by which we will refer to Quintessence in this book, but whatever they call it, astrophysicists now unanimously agree that this incredibly powerful force drives the continuing expansion of the universe, preventing the sum of all matter's gravity from reversing the motion of expansion. This reversal would otherwise cause the universe to collapse in a violent implosion some call "The Big Crunch" which would be its horrific demise. That this does not happen, and is not, happening, is strictly due to the incredible power of the Dark Energy, that is, of God. How strong does something have to be to overcome all the gravity of all the matter in the entire universe? It staggers the imagination.

As mentioned above, scientists have also determined that the amount of Dark Energy in the universe is continually increasing. What is really interesting is that scientists have also discovered that the sum total of conventional matter and energy in the universe is proportionately decreasing. What science does not yet understand is how this happens. This book will advance the idea that this changing ratio of decrease in matter/energy on the one hand, and an increase in Dark Energy on the other, is a confirmation of the Great Cycle of Creation. Thus, life and other processes are continuously, if incrementally, converting matter and energy back into consciousness, restoring to the Dark Energy, that is, to God, what He gave in the creation. This Great Cycle, which began with the Big Bang, will only be completed when the universe is again pure consciousness, that is when all matter and energy have been transformed back into Dark Energy and there is again only the unity of God remaining. This is how the universe was before the Big Bang, just God by Himself existing as pure consciousness. At the end of this current cycle, He will again exist in His complete entirety, and just perhaps, He'll be mulling over the idea of doing it all over again!

Interestingly, as we'll see later, there is a scientific theory called Conformal Cyclic Cosmology that postulates exactly that, in other words an endless series of Big Bangs, each launching a new eon and a new creation.

Can this view of God, and our relationship to Him as givers of consciousness in the Great Cycle of Creation, help to answer any of our more personal questions? One of the most important aspects of any religion is to provide answers, and if possible, comfort, regarding what comes after death. Wouldn't it be nice, especially for religious skeptics, if science could actually help us to find rational answers to this most irrational mystery? And wouldn't it be even nicer it those scientifically-based answers did provide a vision of a life-after-death experience that was positive and comforting?

Towards this end, we will see that there are religious inferences we can make from Science's recent discoveries regarding, of all things, black holes. Most interesting is the proof, coming from studies of these cosmological monsters, that information of any sort cannot be destroyed, even in one of the most cataclysmic of cosmic events, a star or planet being sucked into a black hole. By information, the scientists mean every detail about every atom and every subatomic particle, including their position, their state, their motion if any, their relations and interactions with each other, their energetic states, and all else. This was the conclusion of the famous "Black Hole War" between the two great scientists, Leonard Susskind and Stephen Hawking. Susskind won that war, as documented in his book "The Black Hole War", not just by mathematically proving that all of a star's or a planet's information cannot be destroyed, but also by demonstrating the almost unbelievable means by which it's preserved. This is not a "maybe" thing. Susskind's victory over Stephen Hawking in the Black Hole War proves that under no circumstances can *any* information be destroyed in our universe.

The most important corollary of this discovery for religious thought is that Science has proven, although most scientists do not yet know it, that we do indeed live on after dying. Just as every bit of information in a star or planet that falls into a black hole is preserved for eternity, or at least for the life of our universe, so the unique, intricate pattern of information that comprises each of us cannot be destroyed either, even when a person plunges into the personal "black hole" of his or her own death. This fact will eventually form the scientific basis of an understanding of life after death through the knowledge of the unassailable consequences of the indestructibility of the complete set of information that defines each of us as individuals. We will go into this in much more depth later.

Perhaps now we have planted the seeds of a new understanding of God, the universe, ourselves and our purpose here in light of recent scientific discoveries. By the time readers have finished this book, hopefully they will have come to feel that they've at least seen those seeds germinate, and that the resulting seedlings will provide inspiration for theologians and scientists to take the ideas that are advanced here to the next level and very far beyond.

The important message that hopefully will be made clear is that God's purpose for all of us here on Earth is for us to live and grow spiritually so that we can return consciousness back to Him. Knowing that this is His purpose for us, and hopefully gaining the understanding that all religions can bring our attention to God to augment this process, we can realize that conflict between religions is the greatest possible sacrilege. Thus, almost nothing is as important as harmonizing relations between the world's religions. Later in this volume, we will attempt to demonstrate ways that the world's great faiths can learn from each other, and hopefully learn to respect and even love each other.

2: BEYOND $E=mc^2$ TO THE GREAT CYCLE OF CREATION

Since Einstein, scientists have realized that matter and energy were two forms of the same thing. If there were any doubt of this, it was removed by the mushroom clouds first over Los Alamos, New Mexico, and then with devastating results over Hiroshima and Nagasaki. In each case, massive explosions resulted when a relatively small amount of matter (uranium or plutonium) was converted into an enormous amount of energy.

Clearly, the relationship between matter and energy described by Einstein's famous equation $E=mc^2$ has been proven true, but as the question was raised previously, is this equation actually complete? Is it the whole story? As was suggested in the last chapter, perhaps not, as it fails to take into account the third element of our universe besides matter and energy: consciousness.

Is there another fundamental constituent of the universe along with matter and energy that perhaps should become another term of that equation? Is consciousness the only other thing that could have been converted into matter and energy and then be converted back again, returning to its original state? In this chapter we'll take a deeper look at this very novel and important concept.

Two recent scientific discoveries point toward just such a third basic constituent of the universe along with matter and energy. One of these discoveries is in the area of quantum mechanics, where it has been established that observing a particle's quantum state not only affects it, but actually determines it.

This is such a huge discovery that its enormous ramifications have not yet filtered down through human thought and had the huge impact on other disciplines such as philosophy and theology that they someday will. But this discovery is of the greatest importance because it means that consciousness at last has been recognized by science as a very real component of reality, even a defining influence at the most fundamental subatomic level. If that is so, what might its relationship to matter and energy be? As suggested, could all three, that is matter, energy and consciousness, be different forms of the same thing?

The other great discovery that may relate to consciousness is the existence of "Dark Energy," as introduced in the last chapter, sometimes called the "cosmological constant" and as stated, herein also called "Quintessence." Dark Energy is not matter and it is not energy in the conventional senses of those two words. Yet it is real and manifests as a force so incredibly powerful that it actually overcomes the effect of all the gravity generated by all the matter in the universe, including the dark matter (to be discussed later).

Dark Energy was discovered by scientists trying to measure the rate at which gravity should slow the expansion of the universe. To the scientists' amazement, the data revealed that the expansion of the universe is not being slowed by the incomprehensible totality of all gravity, but rather the rate of expansion is being accelerated by something even stronger. This caused a great deal of head scratching and double checking of experimental results, but the data proved solid.

Imagine an unknown force that is stronger than the combined gravity of all the universes' billions of galaxies, each containing trillions of stars and trillions of planets, not to mention billions of black holes with their incredible gravitational fields and all of what is called dark matter with its strong gravity. Clearly, to counter all this gravity, this must be a force of almost infinite power.

But while Dark Energy is such a powerful force, it works in a very measured way. While it opposes and exceeds the power of gravity on the largest of scales, that of the entire universe, it seems to have much less effect on various less massive scales. On the larger end of these lesser scales, it does not overpower gravity at the level of the individual galaxy, so galaxies can continue to exist as huge concentrations of stars rather than flying apart as they would if Dark Energy had the same effect on them as it does on the universe as a whole, that is, overcoming the total gravity. Within each galaxy gravity overcomes Dark Energy, as it does in solar systems like ours and on planets such as Earth. Consequently, stars can keep their planets in orbit, and planets can retain their moons, keep their atmospheres and attract other objects to their surfaces, including beings such as ourselves! Like so many other aspects of our universe, it seems that the behavior of Dark Energy is at the very least an extremely happy accident.

It might be interesting to juxtapose these new scientific discoveries over the Judeo-Christian story of Genesis and see if the puzzle pieces fit together. As per the Bible, God spent six days, or perhaps six periods of time, creating the universe and life on Earth (and most likely other planets) including us. The first day was a long one. Not only did single-celled or very primitive asexual creatures exist alone on Earth for the first three billion years, the energetic intelligence that animated them to arise from the primordial chemical soup must have existed before that, perhaps from the very instant of the Big Bang about fourteen billion years ago.

How and why can it be said that this "life force" existed before life did? The answer is obvious once it is explained. Remember, this is the force that turned chemical soup into primitive life. But the life force could not do that if it came into existence only after life did — it had to pre-date life to be able to take a hand in its creation. In other words, if this intelligence did not exist in inanimate matter or perhaps throughout space, it could never have been the force that proceeded to animate that same matter in the primordial soup. So consciousness as a quality of existence has been here before life, working as an energetic intelligence from within that primordial, chemical soup to coalesce those molecules into the more complex compounds life needed such as amino acids and nucleotides, and then organizing those compounds into the first functioning cells.

Although the idea that consciousness exists in all matter is unorthodox, it is not novel. In his brilliant discourse, *Science and the*

Akashic Field: An Integral Theory of Everything, French professor Ervin László, who holds a State Doctorate degree, the highest awarded by the Sorbonne, maintains that all matter contains consciousness. In A New Science of Life, author Rupert Sheldrake maintains that what he calls morphogenetic fields exist in a hierarchical order that has driven life through the evolutionary process.

These two authors would likely agree that it makes no sense that even if some creative energy orchestrated the birth of life, that it somehow magically flashed into existence in a certain tide pool to take over its chemical process. Rather, these authors would probably agree with our premise that the creative energy was already there because it was everywhere, and in everything. If this is true, then this most primitive, raw life force may exist in a nascent, inactive state in all matter just as László maintains, even in non-living substances, even though it did take living matter to give it tangible expression.

During that first long day, God caused the Big Bang, infused the resulting universe with the primordial life force, and in the case of our planet, created the first life through the instrumentality of that first energetic intelligence.

As far as our planet's history is concerned, the second, third, fourth, fifth and sixth "days" were epochs of creation during which life perhaps underwent the process of guided evolution. On the seventh day, God rested, that is ceased His orchestration of things, and the universe became a deterministic system modified only by random quantum processes and by the free will of some of its life forms.

What is most compelling about the creation account in Genesis is, in fact, the simple phrase God "rested", not "paused," which would not imply being in any way expended, but “resting,” which clearly does imply an expenditure of energy. That indicates that, according to the Judeo-Christian belief system, God did expend Himself or at least some part of Himself in the creation, resulting in a need to rest, and then in His doing so.

Could it be, as surmised earlier, that God needed to rest because He converted a good part of His own consciousness or essence into matter and energy to form the creation through the Big Bang? It seems likely, because at one instant there was only God and no matter and energy, and in the next instant there was all the energy and matter that was ever in the universe, and perhaps all at God's expense. But in our world, almost everything seems to go in cycles, and the relationship between God, consciousness and the creation may be no exception. It may even be, as stated earlier, that the Big Bang is not unique, that there is a cycle that results in successive Big Bangs initiating entire eons lasting tens of billions of years or more.

Renowned physicist Sir Roger Penrose, for one, believes that data collected by a NASA satellite has provided a glimpse into what may have come before our current Big Bang. Penrose sees this data as proof of Conformal Cyclic Cosmology which says that “our” Big Bang was just one of a series of many, perhaps an infinite series at that, with each Big Bang initiating another "eon" in the history of the universe. But whether the Big Bang happened once or repeatedly, the matter and energy that came into existence had to come from somewhere and something, and the only other major quality of the universe besides matter and energy is consciousness, or Dark Energy, which we are suggesting is a term that means the sum of all the universe’s consciousness acting as an active force, even a willfully active force, much as we imagine or posit God to act.

Earlier we discussed how Einstein's equation $E=mc^2$ is incomplete because it does not include the third constituent of the universe, which is consciousness, proven by quantum theory to be an intrinsic quality as the presence of an observer is a factor in many aspects of quantum mechanics. If God created the universe out of His own consciousness, as we have suggested, then consciousness would by definition be interchangeable with matter and energy. But is that interchangeability a two-way street? If so, then should we look for processes that can convert matter and energy back into consciousness?

Such a process may have begun with the Big Bang, when perhaps as much as 30% of the matter and energy created in the beginning turned into something else, perhaps Dark Energy, almost immediately. Could this be because the raw life force that we have posited to exist within all matter was so incredibly concentrated in the extreme density that existed right after the Big Bang that it reverted back to its original form, or simply put, it reverted back to God?

Since then, the low-level pervasive consciousness that is infused through all matter, that evidently can return back to God very rapidly only at extremely high densities, and perhaps much more slowly under normal conditions in inanimate matter, has been joined by another mechanism that can convert matter and energy into consciousness far more efficiently. And just what might it be that can do that? Could it be life?

It will not be hard to answer that question, because each of us, that is, all human beings, can perform exactly that process. We are physical systems that do turn food, water and air into various forms of life energy, clearly including consciousness, which each of us can experience for ourselves first hand. And as we have discussed, we may be able to return that consciousness to God. While other life forms may not convey such a refined, high-value consciousness, they do manifest various forms of life force, and God's tendrils into them may "harvest" whatever consciousness they do generate for His edification. Assuming that our planet is not the only habitable world in the entire universe, then all the life forms on all the habitable planets in the universe are also turning the nutrients they need to survive into life energies including consciousness, and unless our planet is truly unique, God is also harvesting that energy throughout the universe. The bottom line is that a great deal of consciousness may have been restored to God over the last 14 billion years.

So it appears that returning consciousness to God is what we are for. Our purpose in creation is to turn food, water and air into spirit, and give that to God through our Faith, Love, Worship, Prayer, but primarily just from being conscious. This is the Great Cycle of Creation. The Cycle started when God gave fully of Himself to fire off the Big Bang and bring the universe into existence with all its potentialities, one of which is the provision for some of what He gave to come back to Him. That is what we are for and what all life is for, because even the humblest organisms manifest life out of dead chemicals and various forms of energy, and this brings a small measure of additional consciousness into God's creation which edifies Him. Our human consciousness is vast by comparison, so it may well be that each of us is “materially” significant to God, quite aside from

His love for us. If so, this is one more reason why all life, and in particular all human life, is precious and even sacred.

If much of this is so, then we may have two qualities of the universe that are both increasing: consciousness and Dark Energy. Is it possible that they are one and the same thing? Can it be that the generation of consciousness by life and its conveyance back to God is the same thing as the continuing accumulation of Dark Energy, which now comprises over 70% of all the "stuff" in the universe?

The idea of equivalence between Dark Energy and God is certainly not far-fetched. God is said to sustain the universe. Dark Energy does sustain the universe. The consciousness created by all the life in the universe may return to God, increasing Him. Dark Energy is also increasing. Quintessence, as opposed to "the cosmological constant" is the model of Dark Energy that has variable effects through some unknown mechanism. Clearly, if those variations in Dark Energy exist, they've resulted in a universe that is relatively stable and capable of sustaining life. God could be the willful power also known as Dark Energy that adjusts and applies its strength with marvelously adept variation to ensure the maintenance of our stable, life-friendly and continually expanding universe.

If all this is so, then through its discovery of Dark Energy, science has actually found the fingerprints of God. This in turn gives us a new creation story grounded in the latest astrophysics that also sees God as the willful Creator, and thus makes sense from both the religious and scientific perspectives.

3: THE HOLOGRAPHIC UNIVERSE, THE AKASHIC RECORD AND GOD

Science, in the personages of Alain Aspect, Charles Thorn, Gerard 't Hooft, David Bohm, and Leonard Susskind have developed solid evidence that the three-dimensional space that we see as our universe, as countless mystics, visionaries and philosophers have said throughout history, is in some ways much more than meets the eye. Let's start by summarizing their findings, but please do not expect to fully understand, let alone believe this material yet, until a foundation has been established later in this chapter. Here's the summary, just to set the context for what is to come and perhaps prepare the reader to question and evaluate that information. But let it be added that this is the most startling shift in how we view reality in the history of thought, and this is important: *It has been experimentally verified.*

There is a more fundamental, more real "two-dimensional" holographic reality underlying our three-dimensional universe that has very different characteristics than the world that our senses convey to us as reality. This deeper, more fundamental two-dimensional underpinning "projects" out all the information that defines the three-dimensional space that we experience, like the now-common technology of the visual hologram takes two-dimensional patterns and uses lasers shining through them to project three-dimensional images. The idea that our three-dimensional space is not the most fundamental level of reality is so counter-intuitive that it had to be proven to become acceptable science, and thanks to Mr. Susskind and his colleagues, many physicists now believe that the verdict is in. The new paradigm of the holographic principle envisions a universe that is so very different than what we could ever have imagined. This theory is so mind-bending that even top physicists have trouble comprehending it, but it can be simplified for ease of understanding, and in fact was well set forth for a lay readership in Michael Talbot's excellent book entitled "The Holographic Universe."

Is should not be surprising, that this knowledge, which can bring us so much closer to understanding the real nature of our universe, can help us to better understand its connection to its Creator. It can also help us to understand how we are connected to Him, and also to each other. Regarding our connection to each other, the physics behind this connection is profound in its ability to explain things that have long been regarded by rational people as supernatural and unbelievable. But as our understanding of nature expands, the envelope of what is "natural" expands with it. Now science has provided a foundation for explaining things that have long been unexplainable and even unbelievable, such as psychic abilities and extra-sensory perception (ESP), but more about that later.

The first science that led to the realization that the universe is actually holographic was French scientist Alain Aspect's discovery that certain types of particles, in his experiments they were electrons, exhibited some very strange behavior. They seemed to communicate instantly at a distance, in violation of Einstein's "speed limit" for the universe which is the speed of light. Because it violated Einstein's speed limit, Aspect's observations that changing the state of one electron within an "entangled" pair instantly affected the other entangled electron, was so revolutionary that it threatened to radically rewrite our view of the universe. Now that threat has become a reality.

More recent work has concentrated on the behavior of photons, the particle form of light and other forms of radiant energy. Even before scientists began to close in on an explanation for instant communication, the fact that it clearly existed immediately sparked the search for practical applications. The phenomenon of entangled photons is already being applied to usable technology, including incredibly powerful new computer chips, unbreakable data encryption, and possibly even instantaneous communication at a distance.

According to some sources, instantaneous communication is technically impossible, according to others this has been achieved over distances of many kilometers, and promises to revolutionize the speed of communication. This will be especially useful with space probes in particular, as even the minimum distance between, for example, Earth and Mars is 45 million miles, so it takes a radio signal about 4 minutes for the one-way trip. And four minutes is a best-case scenario, generally at typical distances between Earth and Mars, determined by their different orbital periods, a one-way signal takes from 10 to 20 minutes. Imagine how much easier it might be to control a Mars rover if the steering inputs could reach it instantly instead of taking that many minutes for each input, and just as many minutes for a feedback response. There also, no doubt, will be military uses for instantaneous communication with entangled photons, since it would drastically speed up the "reflexes" of weapons systems, especially those that are space-based.

Whether electrons or photons, what science has learned from observing the behavior of these entangled particles has blown the lid off of our conventional understanding of the universe. In the case of photons, entangled pairs are created when they're simultaneously released from the electrons of an atom as a burst of light. These entangled photons have an amazing connection between them – the polarity of one of the pair instantly affects the polarity of its twin, and this happens irrespective of their distance apart. This effect being conveyed from one to the other violates the axiom of physics that nothing can travel faster than the speed of light. And the information about the change in polarity doesn't just travel from one photon to another faster than the speed of light, it travels infinitely faster than light because it takes no time at all, no matter how far apart they are.

Albert Einstein discovered the possibility of what he called "spooky action at a distance" in his equations, but didn't live long enough to see its experimental verification or to learn what causes it. What causes "spooky action at a distance" is the nature of our universe's underlying two-dimensional "holographic" reality that

Susskind and others have described, explained mathematically, and recently began to verify experimentally. It is not an easy concept to grasp, but fortunately we have the holograms that we see in everyday life to help us to understand how the holographic universe works, and why it can instantly connect distant objects.

The key is the term “non-local” which means that in a holographic “film exposure,” an image is stored throughout the entire hologram, not in any particular area of it. To understand what this means, we can contrast a hologram with a conventional photograph, both taken of two people. In the conventional photograph, you can look at the exposed negative or slide, and easily see that each person exists separately in the photograph. Even in a digital photograph, there are certain bits that represent one person and certain bits that represent the other. If you were to cut the negative of a conventional photograph of two people, you might end up with one person in one piece of the picture, and the other person in the other part. Likewise, a digital image can be cropped because different portions of the data contain different portions of the image.

But in a hologram, the complete image of both people can be found in even the tiniest portion of the hologram, even though under the closest microscopic examination there will be no images of people visible. In fact, the hologram looks like an evenly-textured, lightly-patterned gray surface. But since it’s a hologram, you could break it into several pieces, and each piece would still contain the entire picture including both subjects. The image may not be as vivid when projected from a very small piece of the original hologram, but the complete image can be seen, even from a minute fragment. This is because all the information that forms the picture is stored "non-locally" or throughout the entire image. Thus, the two people in the image are completely intermingled, as if you took a cup of water and mixed sugar and salt into it. Both are still there as discrete substances, and if you tasted the water, you could taste its sweetness and its saltiness, however they two flavorings are completely physically intermingled, and it is the same with the visual elements of the hologram. But, with the hologram, when lasers are applied to the film at just the right angles, they decode the film and project an image of what will now appear to be the two separate people. It is important to note that a hologram also projects its subjects in three dimensions, even though it is a two-dimensional medium. So that is how the common hologram you might see in a display at your local mall or museum works. But what does this have to do with the universe?

Remember the entangled photons and their spooky action at a distance? The only explanation for their behavior is that they are actually connected non-locally, the way that the two people in a hologram would be intermingled. Their seeming existence as fully separate objects is actually just one aspect of their existence. Only by being part of something that encompasses both of them and intermingles them spatially can they be directly and instantly connected at a distance — but how?

Now we have a pretty good idea of how, thanks to the work of several scientists: renowned physicist Charles Thorn, Nobel Prize winning physicist Gerard 't Hooft, physicist David Bohm of the University of London and the brilliant Leonard Susskind, who developed a precise theoretical model for the phenomenon extending from his work with black holes. More recently, physicist Craig Hogan of Fermilab Centre for Particle Astrophysics in Illinois has become convinced that he has found proof of the holographic universe in data from his gravitational wave detector.

What these scientists, and many others, believe is that the entire three-dimensional universe that we experience is enclosed at its farthest boundaries by a two-dimensional structure that functions much the way our pictorial holograms do. This holographic enclosure stores every "bit" of information that represents our entire 3-D universe, dispersed throughout this 2-D "skin." Like our holograms, the information is stored non-locally, which is a key quality because that is the characteristic that explains the behavior of the entangled particles. And also like our holograms, it can use 2-D data to define 3-D objects.

One challenge that the physicists have had to overcome was the fact that a 3-D universe can hold many more bits of data than its 2-D skin can, because volume grows much faster than surface area as an object gets larger, and the universe is so large that the difference between its volume and surface area is enormous. The amount of data that the 2-D hologram and the 3-D universe can each hold is limited by their size because each bit of data can't be represented by something any smaller than what physicists call "Planck's constant" which is the minutest possible "length" in our universe. The physicists' answer, which is supported by Craig Hogan's data, is that our 3-D universe must have much lower resolution than we might otherwise think. The known universe must have fewer bits of information per unit of volume than the hologram does per unit of area. This reduction in the density of the data makes our universe relatively "blurry" and it was this blur that Hogan observed while studying gravitational anomalies. Now Fermilab is continuing to conduct experiments to verify Hogan's ideas and provide a more solid experimental underpinning that offers further proof of the theory of the holographic universe.

For these scientists and many more, the verdict is pretty much in that everything that is, and ever was, is encoded in the holographic boundary between the universe, and… what? If the universe is enclosed within this mega-hologram, what might be on the other side of it? Could the hologram be the interface between "reality" and God?

For a possible answer we can turn to the world's oldest religion, Hinduism. Hinduism describes what is called the Akashic Record which is a non-physical plane of existence that contains the entire history of the universe including all human experience. We can also reference the Bible, which talks about The Book of Life in which everything is written. Another Judeo-Christian term is The Book of God's Remembrances. The Akashic record has also been referred to as "the cosmic mind" and "God's eye." But while religious and mystical traditions are rich in references to the Akashic Record, do any scientists see its possible connection to the holographic universe?

Again we can return to Ervin László, who said in his *Science and the Akashic Field: An Integral Theory of Everything* that the Akashic Record is the embodiment of the universe's collective consciousness and both are also the same thing as the hologram that encloses the universe and stores all of its information. It is interesting that László was in close and frequent contact with David Bohm, one of the first scientists to propose the idea of the holographic universe.

Many practitioners of various religions in Greece, Egypt, India as well as Christians, have claimed to be able to access the Akashic Record. Mystics such as Rudolf Steiner and psychics such as Nostradamus and Edgar Cayce have claimed that it is the source material for their revelations. It is likely that the myriad cross-cultural and cross-religion references to something such as the Akashic Record are actually references to the great hologram that science is coming to believe contains the entire data set for the universe. It appears that science has discovered the place where literally, all is written.

While the Akashic Record almost certainly refers to the holographic universe, it doesn't address all aspects of it. It deals with how it stores all the information in the universe, but it doesn't address how it projects our three-dimensional reality from its two-dimensional structure. One can't help but to remember Plato's Allegory of the Cave for a philosophical reference. In this allegory, a group of people are chained inside a cave facing away from the entrance with a blank wall in front of them. Outside of the cave is a fire, and between the fire and the cave entrance, people walk by carrying various objects, casting their shadows on the blank wall. All that the people in the cave can ever see are the shadows on the wall, so they have no idea that these shadows are not actual reality. What is most striking about Plato's allegory is that while he is correctly alluding to a deeper level of reality than that which is apparent, he has the dimensionality of the two levels of reality reversed. He has a "real" three-dimensional reality with a two-dimensional projection being perceived as reality. We now know that the reverse is actually true!

Some interesting conjectures arise from the fact that all people are intermingled in the hologram since the data that comprises each person is stored non-locally. This means that everyone is not just connected, but are literally occupying the same space, that is, we are all completely overlaid amongst each other. In his informative book *The Holographic Universe*, author Michael Talbot proposes that this non-local overlay provides an explanation for telepathy and other psychic phenomena. He also proposes that the idea that the holographic record contains data on all that has ever happened could explain people's perceived memories of past lives. According to Talbot, it isn't that people have experienced any particular past life or series of past lives, it's that they can experience any past life or lives, as all are available within the hologram, or you might say, within the Akashic Record.

If in fact we are all completely overlaid and thus connected, there are a great many implications. It can explain the feelings of compassion and empathy that we feel. From a holographic perspective, empathy becomes something real, not something that we imagine, so when we think that we're feeling the emotions of others, we well might actually be feeling them. The enduring bonds of love can now be seen as a real connection, more real than the physical bodies where we posit them. Even physical attraction, which sometimes seems to be felt simultaneously by both people almost telepathically, is easily explained if people are actually connected non-locally within the vast, great hologram.

With an understanding of the holographic principle, the military's decades-long obsession with remote viewing doesn't seem quite as preposterous, and our own quasi-psychic experiences such as déjà vu are more easily understood. But do the implications of the holographic principle manifest in our daily lives? Are there everyday things we do that reflect on this underlying reality?

4: THE HOLOGRAPHIC PRINCIPLE IN EVERYDAY LIFE

Does the effect of quantum entanglement extend beyond the sub-atomic domain into the everyday world we experience in our daily lives? Since all the data for us, everything we experience and everything we do is stored non-locally in a holographic substrate, entanglement is certainly possible in our day-to-day lives.

Physicist Paul Davies, in his brilliant book *The Mind of God*, explained the basic physics of quantum entanglement so well and so simply that even to paraphrase would be a disservice to the reader. Furthermore, when reading about something as fundamentally startling and unbelievable as the proven realities of quantum entanglement for the first time, or in fact to see it referenced in any way, it is nice for the material to come to us with the authority of a world-renowned Ph.D. physicist. So here are some of Paul Davies thoughts on the subject of quantum entanglement:

> In quantum mechanics, two subatomic particles can interact locally and then move very far apart. But the rules of quantum physics are such that, even if the particles end up on opposite sides of the universe, they must still be treated as an indivisible whole. That is, measurements performed on one of the particles will depend in part on the state of the other. Einstein referred to this nonlocality as "ghostly action at a distance" and refused to believe it. But recent experiments have confirmed beyond doubt that such nonlocal effects are real. Generally speaking, at the subatomic level, where quantum physics is important, a collection of particles must be treated holistically. The behavior of one particle is inextricably entangled with those of the others, however great the interparticle separations may be.
>
> This fact has an important implication for the universe as a whole. If one were to pick an arbitrary quantum state for the entire cosmos, it is probable that this state would represent a gigantic entanglement of all the particles in the universe.[2]

If the connections between us and everything that we see, hear, feel, smell, and taste are in fact built in to the universe through it being one "gigantic entanglement" and thus everything is truly connected, then we can view sensory experience in an entirely new way. First, we can surmise that to be conscious of something is to connect to it directly by becoming aware of our entanglement with it. Consciousness, then, is entanglement! To "know" an object or even a person is to be aware of the mutual entanglement that is a very real connection. This may be particularly true in the Biblical sense of the word! To love is to be entangled, to feel empathy for another person is to be entangled, and sympathy truly felt is entanglement of the most profound sort and the highest order.

In fact, all forms of awareness represent various means of focusing on aspects of our general entanglement with everything there is. That means that the mystic's feeling of oneness with the entire cosmos is not spiritualistic mumbo jumbo, but very real and entirely factual. However, probably due to the evolutionary advantage of sharp focus on the objects of our attention, we generally limit our connection, rather than to the entirety of the infinite entanglement, to particular and currently useful areas of interest. Our senses then can be seen as guides to direct this capacity for entanglement. We can really "know" what we're seeing, and the entire optical mechanism, with its incredible capacity to seemingly create a highly-detailed and very realistic simulation within the brain, actually works much more simply and with a far more reasonable amount of mental bandwidth.

Of course, only we civilized, scientifically educated people have ever "learned" to see sensory experience as simulation. And what a simulation it would have to be, with massive amounts of data processed at an extremely high resolution and frame rate, and in 3-D at that! Primitive people were never weighed down by this misunderstanding, actually thinking that they were directly experiencing what they saw, heard, touched, smelled and tasted. Only now is science, with its discovery of entanglement, giving us a way to return in a scientifically-grounded understanding of the truth of primitive experience.

Viewed through the lens of entanglement, our senses become so much more than a data base for impossibly elaborate simulations. By simply understanding the relationship between awareness and entanglement, we can see that our visual sense, as are the others, is actually a pointer that serves to focus our awareness toward certain portions of our quantum entangled universe, leading to direct "knowing" and direct "experience" of the objects being viewed or sensed. So, all of our senses do nothing more than provide a key to connect us toward a particular focus, so that we can genuinely and directly experience the objects of our senses through the intrinsic entanglement that is a principal characteristic of consciousness. And this is not just true of human sensory experience. Perhaps only through grasping the implications of entanglement can we understand the way some of the amazing sensory phenomena of the animal kingdom can function, such as dogs' and bears' phenomenal sense of smell, enabling them to know where something is by ingesting only a very few molecules. Or bats using sonar to navigate in the dark just as well as other creatures use sight to direct themselves. A few molecules, a few bits of data, and the "knowing" of entanglement makes it all come into focus.

Positing non-local connection within the world of everyday human experience can explain much. It can help us to understand many things we do, sometimes without knowing why, and many things we feel, sometimes without knowing how. This writer came to realize the ubiquitous extent of our non-local experience and interactions while watching, of all things, a tennis match,

The match was a quarter-final at the Australian Open between Rafael Nadal and David Ferrer. I noticed that both players, without exception, would repeatedly bounce the ball they were about to serve, and each time they bounced it rather than striking or just forcing it down as if dribbling, they would instead briefly hold it before bouncing it again. Watching other games, both men's and women's, it was clear that without exception all professional tennis players perform this same ritual of interaction with each ball they are about to serve. Research revealed that at least one player has even been penalized for an excessive amount of bouncing, as many as 25 times prior to a serve. It didn't seem likely to me that a practice so universally performed would be done without reason. Then it occurred to me: the players were establishing an association, a focus on the quantum entanglement between themselves and the ball, or perhaps between their subatomic particles and those of the ball. This would quite literally give them a "feel" for the ball and help them to apply the subtle nuances of motion that impart fine control of it, as well as perhaps help them to anticipate how it would respond when struck, whether by them or their opponent.

The same seemingly ritualistic behavior is also always performed by basketball players at the free-throw line. Without exception, they will bounce the ball a few times before shooting. In both of these situations, a phrase that comes to mind is one that is sometimes tossed around in the sporting world: "making friends with the ball." Without an understanding of the holographic principle and quantum entanglement, the figure-of-speech of "making friends" with an inanimate object such as a ball would seem to lie somewhere between superstition and delusion. But with an understanding of the holographic principle, what is happening makes sense, they are focusing on their entanglement with that object within the non-local holographic realm, enabling them to actually establish a direct connection with it.

Many other situations seem to perhaps imply a non-local connection. People who control complex, high-performance mechanisms such as racing cars or jet fighters report feeling as if they are "one" with their highly-responsive machines. Is this feeling, so common to highly-skilled drivers and pilots, just an illusory feeling, based on their instinctive, reflexive and nearly instant interactions with their vehicles? Or is it possible that there is a real connection at the much deeper and more fundamental holographic level? Certainly, at the holographic level, non-locality means that without any doubt they are actually entangled with their planes and cars, and thus connected. It would simply be a matter of their skilled "connection" to their vehicle, engendering awareness of the underlying entanglement, enabling them to not just feel as one with their vehicle, but to truly be one with their machines.

The question may not be how this connection is established and experienced, but why it is not experienced more, or even all the time. After all, we are nothing more nor less than creatures living within the hologram, entangled with everything as are all other beings. Everyone and everything we interact with is intimately intermingled with us at that level, like salt and sugar mixed together as a solution in a glass of water. Yet it would seem that a survival advantage may be conferred if an organism focuses on the direct spatial reality of their senses, using only the limited awareness of such entanglement as our senses key us into. In this way, we can easily respond to local events, such as threats or opportunities that might be lost in the insane complexity and clutter of the entire hologram, where we could be aware of everything there is or ever has been, perhaps throughout the entire universe. That level of awareness would not likely make it easier for our distant ancestors to pick berries, hunt rabbits or run from a bear!

Why wouldn't an organism evolve and develop to have the best of both worlds – a primary focus on the spatial world, with occasional access to all the underlying non-local connections? Perhaps some do. This would explain how an entire school of fish can swim in perfect concert, simultaneously executing turns and maneuvers seemingly as one, with no easily understood mechanism for such perfect coordination. The best conventional explanation is that each fish senses its neighbors visually and through the pressure sensitive lateral line on their sides. This could account for coordinated movement of small groups but could not happen quickly enough to enable instantaneous coordination of thousands of fish. So certainly, no mechanism within the rules of our normal spatial reality could coordinate so many fish within the minute time frame required. In large schools of fish, individuals who are far removed from each other and with no visual contact still turn at the exact same time. A similar effect is evident with flocks of birds that sometimes seem to fly in perfect unison. This is also hard to explain with reference only to the rules of the normal spatial universe, but the mystery evaporates if these animals are merely coordinating through the direct connection that, according to the holographic principle, and the mechanisms of quantum entanglement, absolutely does exist between them.

Other examples abound in human experience. Is the mystical closeness of romantic lovers a real connection, a realization of the non-local intermingling of their bodies, minds and spirits? If so, they may be entangled beyond the merely physical! And in general, is love perhaps the ultimate human experience of quantum entanglement? The closeness and empathy that love brings to a couple certainly does feel like a real connection. Many people who have lost family members have stated that they feel as if they've lost part of themselves. By this, do they mean that they've lost something that is part of a more expanded sense of self that includes people with whom they have a holographic quantum entanglement?

Does this connection also extend to the more mundane feelings of possessing or owning something – not to the actual ownership but to the feeling that it engenders? Is the sense that something is "mine" actually grounded in the deepest levels of reality and the most fundamental laws of physics, not just in the illusions of a feeling?

People from natives to naturalists have frequently reported a feeling of transcendental closeness with nature. This profound sense of expansive oneness with nature is certainly one of the draws that bring people into wilderness environments for camping, hiking and rock climbing. Although they certainly do not consciously identify these feelings of connection with something as bizarre as quantum entanglement, that still may be exactly what they are feeling. Many mountain climbers also say that they feel an incredible sense of oneness with their surroundings when they gaze down from a summit.

There is no doubt that the feeling of being connected to something much larger than one's self is uplifting, inspiring, and even mystical. But in the context of the holographic principle and quantum entanglement, this is neither supernatural nor imaginary, but is perhaps a more fundamental and authentic experience than these people's everyday spatial consciousness with its feelings of separation from external objects.

People just driving down the highway, including this author, have another common experience that may have non-local or holographic underpinnings indicating awareness of entanglement. Have you ever glanced over at a driver in another lane, perhaps from the rear and side in what should be their blind spot, and immediately the driver turns and looks back at you? You don't believe that you've done more than shift your eyes and can't imagine that the other driver actually saw you looking at them. It's as if they have eyes on the back of their heads, or as if they somehow feel your attention on them and react to that feeling. If you've had that experience, welcome to the holographic universe and quantum entanglement!

Another common phenomenon that many people experience is intuition or a hunch. This is when we are sensing or even "knowing" something without significant amounts of real evidence or cause for the belief. It's just something that comes into a person's consciousness, and not surprisingly, in the light of the holographic principle, intuition is often very accurate. Many police officers, after years in the field, get very well-honed intuition for things like the identity of an offender, truthfulness of a suspect, or even the veracity of a victim. And it also works in reverse as well. The suspect in turn "knows" that the police officer "knows" and frequently confesses. Another crime solved in the holographic universe.

Then there are dreams. Where do they come from? Why do they sometimes seem to be precognizant? How can they take us to places we've never been? Is it possible that the dream experience, unconstrained as it is by the limitations of our normal waking state, has easier access to the holographic realm, in other words, to the Akashic Record, than is evident in normal spatial consciousness? And in that vein, what about "dream time" as traditionally experienced by Australian aborigines and similar shamanic states reported by other peoples? Have these peoples perhaps not lost so much of their connection to a primal, elemental and more expansive level of human consciousness? What about mind-expansion in general? To just where does the mind expand?

But perhaps the most interesting implications of the holographic principle in everyday life relate to the most universal, ubiquitous and significant event in the life of any person: death, and the mystery of what comes after. What can the holographic principle and the cutting edge physics that brought it to us help to illuminate our journey into the ultimate darkness?

In Chapter 6 we'll take a look at how the holographic principle can shed light on what happens when we fall into our personal black hole of death. But first we'll take a look at something that has been baffling astrophysicists for many years, something that we know is there because it has enormous gravitational force, but is completely invisible in any form of light or radiant energy, the infamous phenomena scientists call dark matter.

5: DARK MATTER VERSUS DARK ENERGY: WHAT IS DARK MATTER?

The nature of what is called "dark matter" is one of the great mysteries currently baffling astronomers and astrophysicists alike. They know with absolute certainty that it exists, but have absolutely no idea what it is. It is evident to them only because it has a great deal of gravitational force, enough to profoundly affect many aspects of our universe. For example, according to CERN:

> In fact, researchers have been able to infer the existence of dark matter only from the gravitational effect it seems to have on visible matter. Dark matter seems to outweigh visible matter roughly six to one, making up about 27% of the universe. Here's a sobering fact: The matter we know and that makes up all stars and galaxies only accounts for 5% of the content of the universe! [3]

Just what is the remaining 95 percent of the universe? As mentioned about, 27% is dark matter. A whopping 68% to 70% of the Universe's total stuff is Dark Energy, which has no mass, weight or gravity. In fact, Dark Energy has a repulsive force that can overcome gravity on the scale of the *entire universe* keeping it expanding instead of falling into itself in what is called "The Big Crunch." But fortunately for us, the repulsive power of Dark Energy is weaker than gravity on smaller scales, even as large as an individual galaxy or especially important for us, in a typical solar system or on a planet such as ours.

How do scientists measure Dark Energy if it has no mass or weight? The measurements were most recently confirmed by an international project called the Dark Energy Survey (DNS). It employed purpose-built equipment to provide data for this determination. Here is one item from the CERN website:

> The primary instrument for DES is the 570-megapixel Dark Energy Camera, one of the most powerful in existence, able to capture digital images of light from galaxies eight billion light-years from Earth. The camera was built and tested at Fermilab, the lead laboratory on the Dark Energy Survey…
>
> To learn that Dark Energy existed, we measured the structures within the universe (e.g., galaxies and galaxy clusters), the geometry of the universe (e.g., the Cosmic Microwave Background) and the expansion rate of the universe (with supernovae). In the Dark Energy Survey, we measure different versions of all of these phenomena.[3]

In order to maintain the universe's expansion, Dark Energy must not only overcome the gravity of all the visible matter in the universe, but also that of the dark matter with has six times as much gravitational force. So Dark Energy is extremely powerful, and absolutely necessary for the universe to survive instead of perishing in The Big Crunch. Dark matter is a more easily measured because it has an identifiable gravity signature.

CERN goes on to give an example of how scientists know that dark matter, and its hugely powerful gravity, do indeed exist, "Galaxies in our universe seem to be achieving an impossible feat. They are rotating with such speed that the gravity generated by their observable matter could not possibly hold them together; they should have torn themselves apart long ago."[3] So what gives galaxies the necessary gravity to overcome the centrifugal force that should be tearing them apart? Scientists say that only dark matter can actually hold all the universe's galaxies together.

So what is the source of dark matter, or rather, what makes the gravitational force that is the only evidence of its existence? This is such a bothersome question that scientists are even positing the idea that matter in another dimension can somehow transfer its gravity from one dimension to another. But we really don't need to imagine something like that, we have a huge amount of matter in our own dimension that is quite capable of projecting the gravity of dark matter\ throughout the universe.

As was discussed earlier, the universe is completely enclosed in a two-dimensional holographic skin or substrate. This substrate is in the business of projecting qualities of every possible kind into our three-dimensional space. Can it also project the gravitational force we attribute to dark matter? If so, the gravity would come from something invisible in our known universe, yet still manifest as a very powerful force. But to have gravity to project if would have to have its own mass to generate it.

According to physicist Leonard Susskind, writing in his fantastic book *The Black Hole War*, “Next imagine a spherical shell of material — not an imaginary shell, but one made of real material—surrounding the whole setup. This shell, made of real material, has its own mass.”[4] And how much mass might that be? It would be a shell surrounding the entire universe, and would have to be continuous. Because holograms store information non-locally, every bit of data in the universe would have to be everywhere in it. This means that it physically stores an almost infinite amount of information. This would imply that it might have an incredibly large mass. The gravity of dark matter is six times as much as the visible universe, and six times the mass of the visible universe is not an unreasonable speculation as to the entire hologram’s mass.

Now if the gravity of that mass is projected into the space of our universe, and remember that everything else in our universe has data that is projected from this holographic substrate, then we have our culprit, the source of dark matter’s gravity, without having to imagine that it comes from somewhere outside of our universe, such as another dimension. Mystery solved!

6: DEATH: THE END OF THE ILLUSION OF SEPARATENESS

If you accept the strong evidence and growing scientific consensus that a holographic structure underlies our universe, you already understand that all the information that comprises *you* must primarily exist in the 2-D holographic skin that encloses the 3-D universe. While you do exist as your familiar 3-D self, all the information that defines that existence dwells only within the holographic substrate. You also should know that your information is stored in that holographic skin non-locally, thus your information is distributed throughout the entire hologram, which is also to say, throughout the entire universe.

Knowing that in fact we are not separate in any way from the rest of the universe, yet also knowing that in our 3-D world we certainly seem to be, raises the quandary of just how authentic is our feeling of separateness? If the underlying physics is clear that we are not really separate, then our feeling of separateness must be a construct in our minds. But why would we labor under such an all-encompassing and completely persuasive illusion? Wouldn't we be more effective if we had instant knowledge of everything in the holographic record, including information on the activities and thoughts of other people, the locations and intentions of dangerous predators, the vulnerability of prey animals, the germination status of seeds recently planted for crops, the real feelings of a potential mate, and a seemingly endless array of other valuable classes of information? But while bombarded by the incredible information overload that would completely overwhelm our ability to assimilate it, we could lose focus on our interface with the three-dimensional "reality" in which we function.

We probably couldn't function nearly as efficiently without the sharp focus that our identification with the three-dimensional world gives us. While our feeling of separateness from the holographic reality is actually an illusion, it is a most useful one without which we would probably function poorly in the 3-D world we see around us. This 3-D world is physically real, but its characteristics are determined by the underlying holographic reality. Our three-dimensional selves are, nonetheless, subject to things and forces in the 3-D realm that have the real capacity to kill or maim or perhaps to please us. Even if the actual underlying data for these events is determined in the 2-D hologram, we would feel the pain and suffer the destruction here in our normal waking reality. Hence, our bodies and brains are mechanisms that preserve the illusion of separateness to enhance our function in the everyday world. But when our bodies are dying, do they then at last lose the ability to sustain the holographic illusion as they lose their other normal living functions?

If so, might death be, among all else that it is, at its core, the end of this illusion of separateness? And with that illusion gone, could death actually be the opening of a door to recognition that we are, and always have been connected to everything there is in the holographic record, including our departed loved ones, our most cherished experiences, and even God Himself?

To help us understand what happens at death, we might start by looking at some other scientific discoveries made by Leonard Susskind and popularized in his book *The Black Hole War*. The book chronicles his conflict with another great physicist, the famous Stephen Hawking, over whether information is destroyed or instead somehow survives when a star, or a planet, plunges into a black hole. Hawking maintained that a black hole would destroy everything about the star or planet, including obliterating all the information contained within it. In this sense, information means all the particulars about every atom and subatomic particle within it, including their quantum states, as well as all the large-scale data describing large scale characteristics that the status of its subatomic constituents determines.

Susskind, on the other hand, considered all information to be inviolable links in the chain of cause and effect or "quantum determinism" and thus as indestructible as the future effects with which they're "pregnant." Quantum mechanics maintains that all information about a system is encoded within it. Quantum determinism means that given the existing information about a system's state, the system's future changes are uniquely determined.

Susskind found that when an object falls into a black hole, its information remains encoded on the outside radius, what is called the "event horizon" or the point at which the black hole's gravity becomes irresistible. While the matter from a planet or star continues on into the black hole increasing its mass, its information is preserved in a "film" as Susskind calls it that exists at the event horizon. Since this film is two-dimensional, although spherical, and the information being described is three-dimensional in nature, the storage within the film must be holographic. This led to Susskind climbing on board with Bohm and others who were advocating what Susskind would call his "holographic principle." Susskind basically extended the holographic behavior at the event horizon to include all matter in the universe, and the films around black holes to be sharing their information-retaining function with the huge holographic film around the entire universe. Information, then, is stored at the universe's boundaries, whether at its farthest extreme or at the boundaries that separate conventional space from whatever's within a black hole. For the mathematically inclined, this means that the area within a black hole's event horizon is topologically "outside" of the universe.

Like stars and planets, people are also objects that contain information. In fact, it is the incredibly intricate structure of the information we contain including every quantum state within our physical matter and all of our energetic activities that makes us the unique individuals that we are. This includes the information relating to our consciousness, which is every bit as real as any other presence in the universe such as matter or energy. So, if we are in every way the sum of all of our information, from the chemical activity within our cells to the electrical activity within our brains, why would this information be any different from any other information in the universe? Why would living systems be the one type of object that can violate the principles of quantum determinism? How can they, among all the things in the universe, lose their information content under any circumstances, even upon death? How can death do to a human personality or soul what the unimaginable power of a black hole can't do to a star?

The position of this book is that death can't destroy this information, built up over a lifetime of experience, learning and refining of our conscious faculties. The corollary of Susskind's work is that the information describing a living system must be retained in the holographic film surrounding the universe, even though the changes in that information that accompany death are also stored there. But that doesn't matter if the information describing the person while they are living continues to exist within the holographic film forever – or at least until the end of our universe.

Susskind is certainly one of the greatest living physicists, but he carefully avoids any discussion of consciousness, religion, or even the impact of his Holographic Principle in the field of biology, quipping in an interview published in the California Literary Review that, "I'm not a licensed cognitive scientist." But many others such as Ervin László are not so shy to take on these issues. Some of these open-minded scientists are now grappling with the implications of the Holographic Principle on the relationship between the universe and consciousness, a quality of the universe that now seems, to many thinkers, to be an integral part of its overall makeup, not a random artifact of biology.

Some, such as László, see the holographic structure as equivalent to a universal or collective consciousness. If that is the case, then the element of consciousness within us would also be part of our overall data set. Our memories, experience, even our sense of self would then be preserved along with the rest of the information that defines us; in fact, it might be the type of information most native to the holographic storage medium! This is especially true if the hologram is indeed equivalent to some kind of universal consciousness such as Carl Jung's over-soul. This mechanism would provide for the first time, a scientifically-based scenario for life after death. But what would this life after death be like?

Here we must enter the realm of pure speculation, but we can be guided by the rich literature associated with the near-death experience (NDE). As most of us know, there is a long-held tradition that someone facing immediate death, and we obviously wouldn't have heard the account unless they didn't end up dying, sees their entire life flashing before them. This is what might be expected as one begins to lose their sense of separation from the hologram and experiences it directly. Simply put, this vision of their entire lives is a glimpse into their realm within the holographic Akashic Record.

It appears that the mechanisms that create the illusion of separateness must begin to shut down before death, allowing us to get a brief but still fully-conscious experience of the great hologram. To be clear, this is not something that happens because we are dead, it's something that happens because we are still alive, but our brains stop performing the complex activities that create the illusion of separateness. Thus, they would also stop playing whatever role they do in generating our perception of the three-dimensional projection from the two-dimensional hologram.

Once we're released from these illusions, we experience the underlying and more fundamental reality of our existence as our connection to everything and everyone within the hologram, beyond space and time as we knew them. Then, when physical death comes and the body drops away, the transfer to the holographic afterlife has already occurred.

Since the re-focusing of our consciousness toward the holographic reality and away from the three-dimensional illusion, can begin to take place before physical death, if the process of dying is interrupted, and the person revives or continues to live, then the mechanism that creates the three-dimensional illusion, central to normal waking consciousness, switches back on and there is a return to normal life. But the person remembers this profound near-death experience. The very real NDE they've just had is perhaps the most real experience a person can have, because during it they've lost the illusion of separateness and became conscious of the deeper reality within the hologram. Later, the experience becomes a dreamlike, but still vivid, memory.

It's also possible that the experience of immersion into the state of connectivity can be visualized in ways that are unique for each dying person. Perhaps some visualize that they're crossing a river, some see a great white light, some see their departed relatives welcoming them to the other side, and some may even meet St. Peter at the Pearly Gates! But these are all representations that the human mind, still in its physical existence since this process precedes complete physical death, creates to give a visual interpretation to an unfolding experience that is completely foreign, abstract and actually beyond the visual sense. It is also very likely that the mind might be guided by the person's religious beliefs, and that as it creates its own pre-programmed dreamlike interpretation of their consciousness connecting to the hologram, visualizing cues from the person's beliefs, to provide a familiar contextual framework to a most unfamiliar event.

The mechanism that creates this visual representation of the opening of consciousness to the holographic reality, that is to everything that is or ever was, is probably the same mechanism that creates normal dreams while we sleep. This can't help but remind us of Shakespeare's take on death in Hamlet's soliloquy. "To die, to sleep; To sleep, perchance to dream—ay, there's the rub: For in that sleep of death what dreams may come, When we have shuffled off this mortal coil…"

Our ability to dream is a highly creative faculty, quite capable of generating any visuals whatsoever. Thus, the dreamlike state as we transition to death is probably guided by our religious beliefs, or other preconceptions, creating a comfortable or familiar wrapper for the experience of opening ourselves to what had heretofore been only in the background, our connection to the universe's great hologram.

But what about people that experience a violent, and especially an instantaneous death, that deprives their mind of any chance to create the transitional dream that bridges people from this life to the hereafter? What might people who die like this experience?

The answer would seem to be that they are immediately immersed in the holographic film, and it is no doubt a harsher way to enter than to experience some sort of transition. But ultimately, they will begin to experience exactly what they would have had they died more slowly and had the luxury of a transitional experience.

Does the idea that everyone enters into the hologram upon life's end mean that there is no reward or punishment after death? Not necessarily, because not only may we continue to relive our entire lives, we will likely do so with full knowledge of their real impact on others, we should even be able, or even be compelled, to feel the emotions, whether joy or pain, of the people we've touched.

This could be incredibly rewarding for someone who has lived their life well, but it could just as well be agonizing for someone who caused a great deal of pain in other people with whom they will henceforth be fully co-mingled. But why would anyone be drawn close to any particular person within the almost infinite amount of data in a hologram that represents the entire universe?

The answer to this question is that although everyone's essence is stored non-locally throughout the hologram and there are billions of individuals just from this planet alone, closeness or connection to certain people such as relatives, spouses and friends is also part of the data sets of all people. This should create a lasting affinity for people who exist within each other's data sets in the afterlife.

But this affinity would not exist with people with whom one has no experience. This affinity would also extend to people that we've hurt or that have hurt us, hence there is a likelihood that we will experience the pain that we've caused others, and that others will experience the pain that they've caused us.

Our connections with spiritual teachers are also part of our overall data sets, so within the hologram our connection to Jesus, for example, can become fully realized. But the connection to Jesus, if we are to believe the claims of Christianity, is unique and special and supposedly confers certain benefits in the hereafter. Is this impossible? Not at all, with Jesus as a primary essence and shared data set with which to co-mingle, there could perhaps be help from Him to engender a great deal of direct interfacing with God, as well as bounteous love, warmth and comfort.

But anyone who has opened their own door to God will take that connection with them, and God's love will be with them forever. Those who have not found God, or who have been unable to, connect with God in their mortal lives will finally "meet" Him, and they will then be aware of their entanglement with God, and this could become a positive component of the post-death holographic experience.

The knowledge that we do not perish at the time of death, but live on in a far more genuine and complete existence than what we knew as "living" beings should be comforting to many, although no doubt it will be confusing to some. But unlike all previous explanations for life after death, this understanding is based on very recent scientific breakthroughs that are becoming widely accepted by leading physicists. Without this recent science, this explanation of what happens after death could never have been imagined or proposed, at least by this writer.

In no way does this information contradict any religion's explanation for what happens upon death. It merely provides a scientific underpinning to explain why the concept of an afterlife is genuine, and perhaps why good people will have a pleasant afterlife and "bad" people will have some issues to work through.

7: NEW SCIENCE FROM OUR OLDEST FAITH

Hinduism is the oldest of all the world's major faiths. It is the product of an imperfect but important civilization that has preserved its ancient wisdom and knowledge for millennia. Hinduism's *modus operandi* is to master the energetic system that bridges the boundaries of soul, mind and body while kicking the doorway to God wide open.

Among Hinduism's many precious gifts is perhaps the most coherent and accurate view of the architecture of our inner experience, call it the spirit, soul or psyche. But semantics aside, the Hindus have given us a way to understand our own inner selves that is easy to experience and evaluate by just taking note of what one feels and where one feels it.

It is not hard to see that the human being has at its top end, the head, its mental faculties, where we experience thought, discernment and free will. At the other end our bodies, are our genital region and below, where we experience "lower" functions and feelings such as sexual desire. In between, toward the center of our bodies, are the seats of our emotions, for example the "heart" area where we feel love and the solar plexus, where we feel greed, hunger and the satisfaction of a hard day's work.

Starting with these three general areas and the self-evident differences in what they represent, we can begin to look more closely at the seats of all of our drives, emotions and faculties. It will be possible for us to easily observe within ourselves the centers of these feelings and faculties to develop a picture of how they're structured, where they're sensed within the body, and how they interact to form each of our unique personalities.

Ancient traditions from the Hindus to the Hopis tell us remarkably similar information about these centers of our sensations and emotions, although the Hopis don't count the lower two, probably because they are perhaps the least spiritual. The Mayans also refer to these centers in their scripture the *Popul Vuh*.

But it is the Hindu tradition that provides the clearest and most complete picture, with accurate description of the seven centers of consciousness in the body. They all have location and unique functions starting at the base of the spine and ascending up the body to the crown of the head. All have important purposes and functions, and all can drive behaviors, each sending their own signals to the brain that are interpreted as feelings, drives or urges. In an emotionally, mentally and spiritually healthy person they work in concert to cue what we might see as normal behaviors, but when the lower ones drive behavioral choices, the result can be abnormal, even pathological, behaviors. When the highest centers drive behavior to a greater degree, the person can be unusually moral and spiritual.

You might view these centers of consciousness or *chakras* as they are called, as spiritual radio receivers that tune into what the Judeo-Christian Bible in Revelation calls the "seven spirits of God." Each of these spirits is an emanation from the Divine that enters into the dynamic of our spirit/mind/body complexes, each via a particular center of consciousness, or chakra. They each can play a role in various life processes, drives, feelings and behaviors. The more primitive of the Divine spirits of the lower chakras may at times not seem so Divine, because they are so prone to misuse and abuse in many people, but life on Earth, its creation, development and continuance, would not be possible without them. The higher centers are more easily associated with our spiritual selves as we will see.

The knowledge of these centers and other features of our spirits' architecture is the great gift of the Hindus to the entire world. The following chapter is really an extension of this one, but for clarity it has been presented as its own section.

8: THE SEVEN CENTERS OF CONSCIOUSNESS

Rather than start with the highest or lowest center of consciousness, we'll look at them in an order that's much easier to understand and more verifiable by common experience. The most storied of the centers of consciousness and one that we can all understand is the "heart." This is not the pump that sends blood throughout the body, this is an emotional and spiritual center that is one of the most popular subjects in poetry, literature, popular songs and every day culture.

The Fourth Center of Consciousness: The Heart

Everyone has loved someone or something in their lifetime. We've loved parents, siblings, spouses, children and of course pets. The associations between the feelings of love and the heart area is both ancient and accurate. Whether we're talking about romantic love, platonic love, family love or even love of country, the feelings are never described by anyone as being centered anywhere else in the body than the heart. Feelings in the heart are also well-known to soldiers, who truly love their platoon buddies and fight for them as well as for country or flag.

The origin of our word "courage," tells us about its deeper meaning, as a Google search says, "Middle English (denoting the heart, as the seat of feelings): from Old French *corage*, from Latin *cor* 'heart'." So courage is a feeling in the "heart" for caring about something enough to risk danger or death to oneself, motivated by love, whether for country or comrades. Another example is a parent running into a burning house to try to rescue a trapped child. Simply put the English word "courage" derives from the various languages' words for heart.

The traditional figure of speech, "broken heart," also helps to underscore that romantic feelings, in this case the yearnings of unrequited love, are felt in the heart or chest area. The word "heartsick" denotes deep emotional pain. Clearly, according to strong and persistent cultural traditions and our own experience, the heart area is the focal point of some of the most powerful emotions we feel, whether euphorically pleasant like the first love of a teenager, or the heart-wrenching pain of losing a loved one. These feelings can be among the strongest and most profound within human experience, and are the stuff of poetry, literature, drama and even history.

Within western traditions, the feelings of the heart are central to human experience and determine who we love and marry and thus the makeup of our families. They motivate the nurturing of our children and our reverence for our own parents. We can love our longtime friends and this can help maintain cohesive social units, especially in small towns or villages.

But note that the love we feel in the heart is usually associated with someone or something that belongs to oneself: *my* children, *my* wife, *my* comrades, or *my* country. It is even possible to love a material thing such as the house where you grew up or raised your family in. In fact, often nostalgic feelings about something connected to our own experiences can create a tinge of warmth in the heart area. One exception to this is our love for God, which is usually, or at least should be, beyond the grip of possessiveness.

We certainly aren't likely to experience the same degree of warm feelings in the heart for the children, wife, comrades and countries of people we don't know or care about. These feelings are generally reserved for people, places and things to which we're connected, things that are ours.

So we can clearly see that the feelings of the heart are almost always linked to another category of feelings that involve possessory relationships and that reside in a separate, but nearby, chakra or center of consciousness.

The Third Center of Consciousness: Our Connection to the Material World

In Japan, the third center of consciousness, the area we call the solar plexus, is called the "*hara*" and is considered the center of the energetic aspects, even the consciousness of a human being. The Zen Buddhist master Harada-roshi put it clearly when he said "You must realize that the center of the universe is the pit of your belly!"

In the West we're most familiar with the term as part of the Japanese phrase "*harakiri*" which means "stomach cutting" as a form of ritual suicide or *seppuku*. The Japanese didn't do this because of any special desire to carve up their digestive systems, but because they were killing themselves by specifically destroying the center of their being, the *hara*.

In the West, as mentioned above, we refer to the location of the third center of consciousness, or chakra, as the solar plexus, although the term refers more exactly to a group of associated nerves and blood vessels called the celiac plexus or celiac ganglia. However, for our purposes, we've used the more commonly known term solar plexus to describe the anatomical seat of the third chakra.

The third chakra rules our relationship to the material world including desire for power, status and possessions. It is where we feel the desire to become wealthy, land a high-paying and prestigious job, buy an extremely desirable automobile like a Ferrari, BMW or Porsche, or even control a person that we objectify such as a key employee or a "trophy wife."

In the grand scheme of things, the higher chakras should be a greater determinant of our behavior, and as man continues to evolve spiritually someday they will be. But in the here and now, the Japanese are not too far off the mark regarding the importance of the third chakra, the behavior it drives, and the centrality of its influence on our world. From our individual behavior in the cut-and-thrust of the workplace to the dictums of *realpolitik* in international relations, we often behave in accordance with the algebra of power, leverage and control. Is this a bad thing? Sometimes, but it is actually an important stage in our personal and cultural evolution.

One figure of speech that can help us to visualize the third chakra feelings is the phrase "get some fire in your belly" which refers to generating a drive to power, success and achievement. A sales manager might very accurately say this to an underperforming salesperson to try to graphically express the feeling the manager knows has driven his own success, and that he thinks is necessary to drive the success of his employee.

Interestingly, the third chakra is often referred to as the "fire chakra" and the phrase solar plexus implies the heat of the sun. This is the center of our personal physical energy, and everything to which it connects. This chakra gives us the energy, motivation and drive to deal with our material needs from meeting the simple hunger for food to addressing our more complex career, social status, and financial desires and aspirations.

Sadly, this often very constructive energy can also take on a negative or destructive form. This can be as relatively innocent as a young boy shoplifting a toy he wants or as nakedly criminal as a bank robber or con artist trying to take a shortcut to riches. The sin most often associated with a third chakra that's exercising too much influence over an individual is simple greed, but it can even manifest on a grand scale in ways that are dangerous to the entire planet, such as when a dictator like Adolf Hitler tries to achieve world domination. Such impulses do not come from the heart!

Aside from the dangers it can pose, this chakra drives many very positive qualities of people and society such as material sustenance, achievement, success, productivity, and much of our economic activity in general. Beyond any doubt, the third chakra is an important and often positive part of our psychological and spiritual makeup – but a dangerous one as well.

The Second Center of Consciousness: Sexual Desire

The location of the second center of consciousness in the genital area says it all, this is where we feel sexual desire, pleasure and all that goes with it. It is associated with a major nerve center called the sacral plexus. Most everyone has felt the sexual or erotic feelings that radiate out from this center, even seeming to fill the whole body. But in spite of the fact that erotic feelings can become all encompassing, there is little confusion about the localized origin of the uniquely pleasurable and strong sensations that are the fruit of the second center of consciousness.

Few would confuse this feeling, often called "lust" with the distinctly different feelings we call romantic love that are centered in the heart. Lust is a completely separate urge, and although the best couple relationships may be those that combine the two, lust is far more transitory and temporary. Sometimes confused married people equate lust's diminishment with falling out of love, but in reality, that is just a normal readjustment to a sustainable level of sexual desire, and in spite of these changes their heartfelt love for each other may well be as strong, or stronger, than ever. But they break up anyway because the thrill is gone.

If an individual has a very high level of energy and activity in the second chakra, it can easily become dominant over the "voices" of the other chakras and drive behavior with little regard to our higher feelings or needs. If this is the case, a man may spend his hard-earned money on prostitutes, or a man or a woman might destroy a loving marriage and family for the sexual heat of an affair. In some cases, people can live much of their lives, especially when young, acting out their sexual desires and miss, or even intentionally avoid, the opportunity to develop a lasting and loving relationship. They can, for some time, actually avoid the pangs and pains that can come from life's inevitable negative impacts on their higher feelings by submerging themselves into an ongoing series of sexual encounters, the thrill of hooking up.

In spite of the behavioral dangers the second chakra poses, its urgings are obviously the driving force behind reproduction in its most basic form. Observing the behavior of animals from reptiles to the great apes, we can see that sexual behavior hasn't changed that much as life has become more complex and intelligent. It is probably a case of the old adage, "If it ain't broke, don't fix it."

Second chakra urges and behaviors do not necessarily adhere to desirable social norms. For instance, it is not surprising that two of the Ten Commandments are to not covet thy neighbor's wife and to not commit adultery. Any behavior that rates two out of the 10 commandments is clearly something that must be controlled for the good of society. In its most aberrant manifestations, this chakra also drives people to incest and molestation. Once someone, usually a man but lately in the daily news often a woman, begins to blindly follow the pleasurable and exciting urgings of the second chakra, they can be led deeper and deeper down a primrose path, always chasing the forbidden fruit and falling into progressively more destructive behaviors, both to their victims and ultimately to themselves.

Think of the female school teacher who seduces a strapping young male student, or a high school swimming coach who develops a sexual relationship with one of his underage charges. These are examples of someone "listening" to their second chakra instead of their higher faculties.

Although forcible rape usually involves additional aberrant urges, generally a feeling of inadequacy or anger that the individual tries to resolve by assuming a position of power over someone weaker, lust certainly can be contributory to this category of crime. In fact, it's arguable that lust must become part of the mix of feelings for the act to be carried out successfully.

Controlling and managing the primal, and for some, overwhelming, and even frightening power of the second chakra has been one of the primary tasks of culture and civilization since mankind first started wearing clothes. Today and throughout much of history, laws have prevented an individual from openly displaying his or her genitals and some other sexually attractive body parts.

It's no accident that this stricture is solidly cross-cultural. And although of course there are exceptions, there are many cultures living even today with rules mandating severe repression of sexual attractiveness, such as the case of Islam where *sharia* law can require a woman to almost completely hide her body from ankle to face and hair. As most know, Islam also severely punishes sexual transgressions, especially by women, with punishments including stoning to death. This is perhaps the most striking example of how far societies will go to control the sometimes-frightening power of the second chakra.

The Fifth Center of Consciousness: Communication and Compassion

We've all heard the expression that something sad or pitiful gives a person a "lump in my throat." This figure of speech hints that compassion is another localized and unique feeling, in this case radiating from the throat area. It should come as no surprise that these feelings emanate from another one of our emotional centers, or chakras. It is associated with a major nerve complex called the cervical ganglia medulla plexus.

The fifth chakra is the seat of our capacity for sympathy, empathy, compassion and also pity. And while those feelings can be evoked for loved ones for whom we have fourth and third chakra attachments, they are also triggered in cases of people or even animals with whom we have no family, romantic, or other pre-existing emotional or possessory relationship. While it would be highly spiritual to love all mankind, it is much more likely that we really don't. However, compassion is different.

We can have *compassion*, not just for complete strangers but even for people we've never met or animals that we only see in pictures. Examples come to us on our television screens or arrive in our mail boxes on an almost daily basis, such as the mailer or TV spot picturing the pathetic image of a starving young girl, eyes bulging and belly distended. That these ads are cost effective is as clear as the fact that charities are soliciting funds to feed hungry children. Or recall the ubiquitous television spots by animal rights and anti-vivisection organizations that show laboratory animals undergoing what appear to be agonizing experimental procedures. It's enough to make you want to make donation on the spot. That's the power of the fifth chakra.

We probably don't really love the starving child, we most likely don't love the tortured animals, but these images certainly do make us feel something. That "something" is the emotion we call compassion, or in its extreme and often dysfunctional form, pity. Evidently, that feeling is strong enough to make us overcome our materialistic third chakra desire to retain our money, and instead drives and inspires us to mail out a check or phone in a credit card number. Clearly compassion is a strong enough feeling to serve as an effective call-to-action for a financial donation, at least for a significant number of people. If it weren't, the highly-paid advertising experts implementing these fund-raising campaigns for the charities wouldn't be creating and mailing all those millions of flyers and buying all that expensive television time.

So clearly, compassion can *for some* be a very strong emotion, at times strong enough to drive our behavior. Unfortunately, although this chakra should be actively sending messages of compassion to the brain in all people, in those who are badly dissipated there is no energy to feed it, and it is reduced to a dim glow, incapable of producing a healthy response even to what should be the most moving of stimuli. If it was always up to speed in everybody, there would be less cruelty, less crime, less emotional abuse at home and in the workplace, and the world would be a much better environment in which to live. If this were the case, the fifth chakra would be working in concert with the fourth chakra in fulfillment of the Bible's commandment, present in both the Old and New Testaments, to "love thy neighbor as thyself." And it doesn't even have to be a neighbor, or a friend or any other noun that can be preceded by the word "my." And oh yes, sorry Bible, this kind of broad-spectrum positivity doesn't come from love, but from compassion.

Earlier it was said that as we go up the body to chakras at physically higher locations, the emotions they radiate are also of a higher quality. Is compassion really higher than love? It *is* higher, and thus more spiritual, because it is a form of caring for others that is not linked to something objectified as being "mine." There is no linkage to possessory feelings unlike there is with 4th chakra love. Thus, it's not so literally self-centered and is much more about the "other" being.

Love, especially when strongly mixed with possessory feelings as it so often is, can motivate jealousy, violence, even war. Think of the battle in Homer's *Iliad* which was brought on by a King's love for his beautiful wife Helen of Troy, the face that launched a thousand ships. Violence and especially warfare is seldom motivated by compassion, although there are instances where a compassionate rescue operation appears to bring about war in the interest of humanitarian values. In such cases, looking more deeply, another economic or political cause often lurks beneath the surface, and compassion can be seen more as a rallying cry and less as a reason.

But compassion certainly can drive killing, under several circumstances. The most obvious is the "mercy killing" in which horribly suffering people or animals are "put out of their misery" or subjected to "assisted suicide" for purely compassionate reasons. In the case of animals, this is an almost universal practice, but in the case of humans it may not always be legally or socially acceptable. However, even those who condemn these practices would not likely find them morally reprehensible.

The fifth chakra is also the seat of communication, and its associated physiological feature, the cervical plexus, includes some of the nerves that go to the ears. It is physically near the organs of speech and according to tradition, its influence helps empower truthful speaking and effective oration, but unfortunately not always at the same time!

The fifth chakra is the lowest of the chakras that might be considered to be connected to the spiritual world rather than the physical. This is because its drive toward compassion is not generally linked to issues of the self. It also has a role in dealing with things of a vibratory nature including speech and hearing.

Consequently, it is the physical area where we must voice our prayers and our chants, issuing our outward manifestations of our reverence for God, no matter what our religion is. In biblical terminology, it is where we are receptive to what Genesis calls "the Word" which is the Holy Spirit of the Trinity. In the Hindu belief system it is where we can connect to the sacred "Aum" vibration that is a manifestation of God's driving force behind the continuing existence of our world. As science comes to a better and deeper understanding of the implications of the fact that matter is actually made of vibrating energy in the form of waves, our knowledge will come closer to an understanding of what the Bible means by "the Word" or the Hindus mean by the sacred "Aum."

But like most of the other centers of feeling, the fifth chakra can drive problematic emotions and behaviors. Sometimes people use the words "compassion" and "pity" interchangeably, but in fact they represent very different ways of responding to someone else's pain or suffering. Compassion is a feeling of connectedness to the other person, as is empathy, where we seem to share their feelings, in a way that can drive us to want to help them. We can literally manifest what we sense to be their feelings in our own emotional centers and feel them in our own bodies.

Pity on the other hand has within it an element of condescension that places us "above" rather than alongside and connected to the other person. This separation can even be judgmental and generally makes pity unlikely to drive helpful behavior. Even what we call "self-pity" implies an internal separation in our psyche that is almost paralyzing, as in the phrase "wallowing in self-pity." There is also a sense of excessive or maudlin sentimentality associated with the feeling of pity.

But in spite of its potential for driving some negative emotions, the fifth chakra generally exerts an extremely positive influence on our behavior and culture. In an emotionally healthy and spiritually aware person, it can influence our personal choices on a daily basis, literally becoming the driving force behind the Golden Rule.

The Sixth Center of Consciousness: The Driver's Seat of the Soul

The sixth center of consciousness is located in the forehead, centered between the left and the right, and vertically situated slightly above the eyes, in fact just a little above the eyebrows. It is the location of our uniquely human consciousness that distinguishes us as

Homo sapiens or "wise man," and it is the end-point where we interpret and evaluate all incoming sensory data. Because it is where we experience the visual data from our eyes, many traditions refer to it as the "third eye" but a better phrase might be "the mind's eye."

It is also where we receive the feelings and interpret the impulses from the other chakras that would influence our behavior. However, we don't feel them in the sixth center of consciousness, we feel them centered in their own localized areas and radiating out. But the part of us that is experiencing all of these feelings and sensations is in the forehead. The other chakras can have powerful influences over this decision-making center, but fortunately, as humans, in the sixth chakra we have freedom of choice so we can decide whether or not to follow any of the urges from the lower chakras, which in animals would likely trigger unfiltered "instinctive" behaviors. Because it is the seat of choice, it is a good thing that it is also the seat of wisdom.

It's pretty easy for anyone to get an idea of where this "sense of self" or sixth chakra is located. Close your eyes and then position the point of your finger near your mouth. What direction is your finger from the part of you that senses where the finger is? Of course it will feel as if it is below, but it certainly isn't below the vast bulk of our bodies. Now move it slowly upward. Only after it is a little bit above the eyes will it feel like the finger is "up" from your center of consciousness. You can then easily move your finger to the left and right to see that "where you live" seems to be along the central axis of the head and just above the eyes.

This center of consciousness in the brow is an important focus of meditation or contemplation for many of the Eastern belief systems and often adherents will turn their eyes upward and inward to concentrate the visual sense on this chakra. After doing this for extended periods of time, the sense of the separation of the left and right eye is replaced by a strong feeling in the central area, as if the eyes are unified into one.

Many believe Jesus was likely referring to the sixth chakra and this effect when He said in Matthew 6:22, "The lamp of the body is the eye, if therefore thine eye be single, thy whole body shall be full of light." Almost identical language also appears in Luke 11:34. And the effect of concentration on the sixth chakra in the various traditions of yoga is to find the white light, what is called illumination. It is probably not a coincidence that these two separate spiritual traditions should use such similar language about something this important.

This chakra uses God's highest vibratory gift as its power source, even higher than the Word or the Aum that drives the fifth chakra. In order to be capable of wisdom, enlightenment and correct decision making, this chakra actually serves as an earthly reflection of God's wisdom and grace. This is why some very learned, spiritually accomplished people, even including some outside of western tradition, refer to it as Christ consciousness. In fact, that is a very appropriate name for it as the Christians believe Christ is the only way to God, and the sixth chakra is certainly the only way to the seventh chakra, which as we will see is our direct connection to God. So the Christian claim that there is only "one way" to God through Christ is in fact completely correct, although their claim to a monopoly over this connection is certainly not. The Christ consciousness of the sixth chakra has been part of God's creation from our very beginnings and is built into our bodies, minds and souls.

Christians believe that Christ has existed along with God for eternity, thus Christ did not come into existence for the first time along with the birth, baptism or resurrection of Jesus of Nazareth. This has been Christian doctrine since the Council of Nicaea and the suppression of the Arian heresy that maintained that Christ was created by God. So, it follows that if the spirit of Christ has always been here and does predate its incarnation as Jesus, and of course the establishment of Christianity, then this "one way" to God is not dependent on the personage of Jesus or the teachings of Christianity. Rather it flows from the grace of the eternal Christ center, the sixth chakra, and thus it has always been, continues to be, and always will be available to sincere, faithful and righteous seekers of God, no matter what holy book sits on their table. It follows that seekers of God have always had to achieve a connection to what the west calls Christ, even though they may have very different names for it, to fully connect to God.

The wisdom of the sixth chakra is superior to the urgings of any of the lower chakras, even those crying out for love or compassion. It's very interesting that the Hindu scripture called the *Bhagavad Gita* opens with a story that makes clear the relationship between the fallible compassion of the fifth chakra and the higher wisdom of the sixth.

A military leader named Arjuna is agonizing on the eve of a great battle about the horrors that the next day will bring. His compassion for his troops, and even for the enemy troops, is overwhelming him. He does not want to commit his troops to the battle, hoping to avoid the suffering, bloodshed and death not only for his own troops but even for those of his enemy. This is a classic example of compassion where the emotion does not require possessory linkage, but is a feeling that applies to all – even the enemy troops. This seems like such a high and noble impulse that it must be morally correct. Or so it seems.

But God comes to him in the form of Krishna and explains to him that there will be horrible consequences and far worse suffering for a great many more people if he does not fight and win. The enemy leadership is truly bent on evil and slaughter, and even the example of his compassion and his evident high moral purpose would not affect their murderous plans in the least. Arjuna's compassionate approach would have been as if the Allies in World War II had ultimately decided that defeating Hitler would involve too much pain and suffering. Certainly, if World War II had not been fought, many soldiers would not have died, but it is reasonably clear, based on Hitler's actions such as the Holocaust, that without his defeat he would have exterminated many times more people who didn't happen to be born blond, blue-eyed Aryans.

Krishna's chiding of Arjuna toward proper action based on the sixth instead of the fifth chakra is a great way to begin a body of scripture, as it demonstrates clearly, and on the highest level, the hierarchical nature of our spiritual centers and the behaviors they engender and how even a relatively positive impulse such as compassion can be terribly wrong when compared to the choices of wisdom. Homo sapiens. Wise man.

Ultimately, the sixth chakra should allow no impulse from any lower chakra to blindly determine behavior, not even the love of the fourth chakra or the compassion of the fifth, let alone the materialistic or baser impulses from there down. Each impulse must be evaluated by this special faculty of wisdom for its impact on the life of the individual and the lives of others, then that impulse must be either ignored or correctly acted out.

Letting any chakra other than the sixth write the story of our lives, unedited, is to open the floodgates to the entire range of impulsive behavior. Clearly, it's of the greatest importance that our seat of choice and wisdom remains just that. It comes down to something as simple as "think before you act." If we *do* think before we act, and if we are guided by our time-tested religious and moral traditions, most of our choices and behaviors will be correct and righteous, and our lives will unfold in the most favorable ways.

The sixth chakra is associated with the hypothalamus pituitary plexus and some say the pineal gland, an organ that is sometimes called the third eye. This nomenclature is not completely far-fetched as the lizard-like tuatara of New Zealand has a pineal gland that literally functions as a third eye with a cornea-like structure, a rudimentary lens, and a simple retina.

But the biology gets even more interesting. There is something in the pineal gland called brain sand which is a gritty or crystalline substance that has an unknown physiological function, but a proclivity for absorbing radio waves. Some scientists have speculated that this substance can tune into some form of electromagnetic vibration or other emission much as the crystal in a child's science project radio does. The pineal gland is connected to the sympathetic nervous system via the superior cervical ganglion and to the parasympathetic system via the sphenopalatine and optic ganglia. The pineal gland is also connected to the central nervous system via the pineal stalk, and additional neurons connect it to the trigeminal ganglion.

In other words, the pineal gland is richly, intricately and directly connected not just to the brain itself but to the three fundamental branches of the human nervous system, sympathetic, parasympathetic and central. Another indicator of the importance of this small "gland," the size of a grain of rice, is the fact that in humans it gets a very profuse blood flow containing the riches nutrient mix available to any part of the body. Its blood flow is exceeded only by that to the kidneys which are in the business of filtering the body's entire blood supply.

A Greek physician named Herophilus may have been the first Westerner to postulate that the pineal gland is the seat of consciousness. Later, the mathematician and philosopher Descartes came to the same conclusion. Another interesting point about the pineal body is that some scientist believe that it is the first gland to become recognizable in human development, taking on an identifiable form after only three weeks of gestation.

Its location is near the center of the brain, and although perhaps somewhat rearward from the location where we perceive our own consciousness, it is very close – remember the little experiment about what is above, below and the left and right of the body's "driver's seat." The region of the sixth chakra not only has clear underlying physiological importance, it is also experientially and intuitively the driver's seat of our soul.

The Seventh Center of Consciousness: Broadband to God

We've all seen Jewish people wearing the yarmulke, a small skull cap that covers the top rear of their heads. Tradition holds that these are worn so that the sensation of their presence draws a person's attention to that part of their body and thus to their God consciousness. Hindus and Sikhs certainly would not argue with this Jewish practice, in fact their turbans are intended to do the same thing in the same way, by being a physical reminder to direct attention to the crown of the head. In other words, it is a strong cross-cultural institution.

The pervasive visual tradition in religious artwork of a halo or glow around the head also relates to the existence and function of the seventh chakra. This halo or glow is a common feature in paintings of Christ, saints or holy men. This tradition is not unfounded as it is the seventh chakra and its association with the brain's cerebral cortex that enables our highest cognitive and spiritual function, our ability to sense the presence of God and to pass on to Him all our experiences and the gift or our consciousness itself in furtherance of the Great Cycle of Creation. According to 40 scientists stating in the New York Declaration on Animal Consciousness (2024), animals from insects to octopuses have consciousness so they too are part of the Great Cycle.

As has been discussed, God is all-pervasive, that is God is everywhere, including within all beings, human or otherwise, as well as within inanimate matter and empty space. Is there any place that someone could hide from God? Of course not, but nonetheless many people, at least at certain times in their lives, do not feel God's presence. This is not because they are incapable, but because their attentions are turned elsewhere or because they do not feel worthy of "facing" God because of conscious or unconscious guilt over the negative actions we generally call sins. But at any time, when we turn our attention "upward," we can tune in to the direct connection that each of us has to our Creator. Why upward if God is everywhere? It's not that God is up, down, or sideways, but that the organ through which we perceive Him is above the "driver's seat" of the sixth chakra. So to our consciousness, we sense God as being "above" because that is where we experience the connection. The seventh chakra is actually a part of God within us more so than simply a part of us. It might be described as God's tendril into our souls and minds.

If the sixth chakra is the wisdom of Christ consciousness and is responsible for our right actions, what benefits does God consciousness confer on us? How differently does someone who has tuned into the ineffable feelings of direct contact with God think, feel and behave?

To understand this, we need to take a very long view of the human experience. After we, as individuals, have perished, after our species has perished, after the planet Earth has been obliterated by the Sun's death throes, how important are all the right actions and good decisions we've made? While they seem, and in fact *are,* important in the here and now, in the grand scheme of things, our lives are like dreams that flash before our eyes for a few years and then are over.

What matters for eternity is our connection to God, and what we bequeath to Him within the Great Cycle, all else is trivial by comparison. At the level of the seventh chakra we genuinely realize that the only thing that ultimately makes a lasting difference is whether we "walk with God." It's this sort of understanding being deeply felt, not just thought, that enabled the Christian martyrs to face even the most painful of deaths peacefully and without losing faith. It is the transcendent objective of Buddhism and Yoga. And it is the final benefit that our sincerely practiced Faiths can confer on us as we each face our own martyrdom at life's end.

True connection to God is the strongest feeling that we can have as human beings, capable of displacing all others, or at least putting them in perspective. It can sooth our pains, quiet our fears, and fill us with a joy or bliss that defies even the worst circumstances in our lives. A materially poor man with a true connection to God is infinitely richer than the monetarily wealthiest man who hasn't been able to open up to God yet.

But how can we reach this level of God consciousness? Do we have to go to Tibet and meditate in a cave with a mysterious guru for fifty years? No, we merely have to sincerely practice whatever religion our families and cultures have taught us and in which we may somewhat believe. If we follow the guidance of our time-honored scriptures and religious practices, and make a sincere effort to choose the actions that elevate us rather than the actions that lower us, we will find love, compassion, wisdom and finally the real consciousness of God that is our birthright as human beings.

It doesn't matter if our religious practices and beliefs include revealed truth or preposterous mythology. It doesn't matter whether we believe the universe is six thousand years old or fourteen billion. It doesn't matter if we think we evolved from monkeys or were created from dust on the sixth day. It doesn't matter if we call the Deity who is Lord and Creator of the universe by the name of God or Allah. All that matters is that our religious traditions guides us to the point where we can sincerely follow the religion's strictures and our own sense of right and wrong, essentially fulfilling what amounts to a rite of passage that makes us feel worthy, then without even knowing the particulars described here or what a chakra is, we can open the door in the seventh chakra and let our connection to God come whooshing in. It happens every day to people all over the world.

The First Center of Consciousness: The Throne of God, Pandora's Box, or Both?

The sacral-coccygeal ganglia lies near the base of the spine, in the region of the bone called the sacrum, really a broadened column of five fused vertebrae. Do the words "sacral" and "sacrum" seem to echo the word "sacred?" The answer, of course, is yes, our word sacrum derives from the phrase "sacred bone." Some sources attribute this word origin to the sacrum having been given special attention during animal sacrifices. Of course, that brings us full circle because this would indicate that those performing the sacrifices already regarded it as sacred!

As Brian Stross, professor at The University of Texas at Austin says in his article *The Mesoamerican Sacrum Bone, Doorway to the Other World*, "Upon finding that some Mesoamerican Indian languages also named this bone with words referring to sacredness and deity, one may well ask why societies distant from one another refer to the sacrum as a "sacred" or "holy" bone." Clearly, this bone being somehow sacred is an ancient belief. What is the structure called the sacrum and why would people believe it to be so holy? And is it really the bone that is sacred, or perhaps something that's part of our spiritual anatomy in that region rather than the bone itself?

The sacrum is a large, shield-shaped bone. It is situated below the lumbar region, so it might also be called the base of the spine. The spinal cord continues through the spinal canal into the sacrum and through it into the coccyx or "tailbone." The sacral nerves exit the spinal canal through bony passages called foramina and interconnect with the massive nerve center called the sacral-coccygeal ganglia.

As we've explored the system of the spinal centers or chakras, we've observed a clear trend. The "higher" aspects of our natures are located progressively farther up the spinal column. Wouldn't the lowest chakra be the home of our lowest urges and emotions? And if the seventh chakra, at the very top of our bodies, is our broadband connection to God, why is this center and its associated anatomical features, located at the very bottom of the spine, called sacred?

The short answer might be that all the chakras are sacred, various aspects of the life forces which are all emanations from God. After all, where else could the energies driving the chakras come from? The fact that most of them can be, and often are, abused doesn't contradict that fact. Likewise, even though our eyes, ears, brains and hands are gifts from God, many people misuse those anatomical features to commit crimes. Clearly, all the chakras are gifts from God, but none of the others are associated with areas of the spine that have been called "sacred" for hundreds of generations or longer. What makes this one chakra so special, so sacred?

Although at first it seems contradictory, the answer does lie in the sequential nature of the chakras, both in their physical placement and in their progressively more refined functions. The key to their underlying processes is that each one is fueled by energy from the one below it, unless that energy is dissipated to the point of unavailability by abuse of the emotional and energetic "voltage" of the center. But if all is well, the higher chakra then receives that "lower" energy and in turn transmutates it into its own more refined essence. Then, the energetic "product" of that chakra fuels the next chakra up, which in turn transmutates that, and so on up to the final gift of higher consciousness of God in the seventh or crown chakra. But this process has to begin with some fundamental life energy, and this is what the first chakra accesses, the raw Divine spark of life itself that was introduced into creation by God on the "first day." The first chakra then is the seat of our unalloyed life force, called chi, prana or, by some western observers, orgone energy or animal magnetism. This is a force more primitive and powerful than even our sexuality, and it is a force we share with all other living beings from the simplest bacteria up to the most advanced mammals.

So to reiterate, without the raw life force of the sacral region, there would be no energy to cascade upwards first into sexuality, then into materialism, then into love, then into compassion, then into wisdom and finally into God consciousness, in the sequential order of this great process of transmutation.

Here the word transmutation is not used by accident or with unawareness of its alchemical connotations. The system of the chakras and their refining of the raw life force all the way up to God consciousness is the true conversion of lead into gold, the true philosopher's stone of alchemy, all of this being code for a very real, natural and fundamental process, the esoteric climb up the 33 degrees of Freemasonry, a degree for each of the 33 vertebra that are within the spinal column.

Calling the sacrum the actual seat of God might be considered an overstatement, but the sacrum and the first chakra do constitute the seat of God's presence within us, and hence it was properly accorded the appellation of "the sacred bone."

But after all, this is the lowest chakra, so is there more to it than that? Can the energy of this chakra, like many of the others, be somehow abused? It certainly can, for within it lies primitive and powerful urges that can stimulate a variety of human behaviors, from benign gender identity and sexual orientation issues to actions generally considered perverted, all the way to some of the most horrific and harmful of all human activities.

To understand this, let's think about what might be more primitive than heterosexuality which has urges and behaviors that are remarkably similar in human beings and in "lower" creatures from apes to alligators. But what about organisms that don't have sexuality, for example one-celled animals like amoebas and bacteria, or even the billions of cells that exist in the very well-organized cellular colony we call the human body? How do they reproduce? The answer as most of us know is that they reproduce by cellular division, by splitting in two. Arguably, since the original cell or organism is replaced by two new ones, these individual animals reproduce through self-destruction or death. For them, reproduction equals death, *eros* equals *Thanatos*.

Many thinkers including Sigmund Freud have observed an association between sex and death, often mixed with large dollops of sadism and/or masochism. But Freud thought that the death impulse was an urge to return to the non-living, inorganic state. He missed the fact that self-dissolution is unarguably the most primitive, fundamental and universal form of reproduction. It's completely unnecessary to inject an "anti-life force" into the human psyche as did Freud, in fact the earliest and most basic life force, cellular dissolution and its reproductive "psychology" is the key to solving this behavioral puzzle.

It is no stretch from here to imagine, as Freud and others observed, just why sadism and masochism are common in individuals whose pathology integrated Thanatos, or death elements, into their erotic and sexual fantasies and actions. The urge toward death or injury is a direct expression of the primordial reproductive process of self-dissolution, in which the "parent" individual is literally severed in half to create new life.

And remember, this psychology doesn't just apply to amoebas and bacteria but to every cell in our bodies. In other words, this energy and its associated process continues to permeate our flesh and animate the lives and reproductive processes of our cells. But generally, this force operates in the background, "experienced" unconsciously at the cellular level rather than as a conscious urging to any behavior.

Now imagine that a person can tune into the feelings of this energy and make the choice to follow the urges that it generates. A gateway behavior that can initiate movement into this area of feeling is what is now called "cutting," in which a person, generally young, makes non-lethal incisions in their own body, usually in the arms.

They are not trying to slash their wrists to commit suicide, or simply to feel the localized pain, but really to feel the powerful visceral sensation that this behavior, hinting at dividing the flesh, brings. What they don't realize, is that this behavior and its accompanying visceral sensation is opening a door to the dark side of the first chakra's feelings. Whether through this gateway or other behaviors, the result is to awaken the feelings that evoke and mimic those of dissolution and destruction that is the climax of cellular life. But now these feelings are made manifest at the level of the individual human being, instead of where they belong, at the cellular level. This stimulus-response loop can gradually self-energize to trigger behavioral patterns such as sadism, masochism, even finding a thrill in the death of oneself or others, and even, in literal mimicry of the schism of cellular division, the twisted excitement that some serial killers find in dismembering their victims.

The energetic intelligence of the first level of consciousness is also un-polarized into male and female genders, so it's eroticism in the human context can be non-heterosexual, in fact according to Hindu and Sikh traditions it is the seat of homosexual behavior. Does this mean that homosexual behavior is wrong or aberrant because if comes from the first chakra? Not at all, in fact on the contrary, it means that it's part of every human being's nature, whether as nascent potential or realized feelings and behaviors. By many indications there are environmental factors or family patterns that can increase the likelihood of overt homosexual behavior, but the potential must be there, and in everyone. Genetic factors cannot be completely causal as they would quickly be selected out of the gene pool since homosexual orientation would greatly reduce reproductive activity.

So is homosexuality any more "wrong" than heterosexuality? Of course not, but complications arise in the effect of abuse of any emotional center, including the first and second chakras. The effect of spewing out the energy of either chakra through excessive or compulsive heterosexual or homosexual behavior that is undirected, unmodified and uncontrolled by the energies of the higher chakras is roughly the same – what we call "dissipation." In other words, there is little energy remaining in the chakra, and thus little available for passing on the next higher chakra and for the cascade of upward conversion to the higher energies. If this upward cascade is not happening, the higher emotions are not so strongly felt. It's important to mention that sexual or erotic dissipation has the same effect on the health of the upper five chakras whether the dissipation occurs through second chakra heterosexual obsessive behavior or taking first chakra homosexual behavior to excess. The result of dissipation at either level is the same, there is very little remaining energy to cascade upwards to the solar plexus, and then further upwards to the heart and the other higher centers.

But on the other hand, anyone who integrates their sexuality into a harmonious, balanced and loving life with strong emotional and spiritual feelings, clearly has not dissipated their energy and therefore has an equal potential to focus on and develop their higher faculties. In fact, especially in comparison to the "Thanatos equals eros" behaviors, the natural behaviors of homosexuality are clearly a highly positive implementation of the first chakra energy.

Although it is a stereotype, there may be some truth to the supposition that homosexuals can have exceptional creative abilities. Is it just because they don't want to work as plumbers that they are some of the best clothing designers, hair stylists, actors, singers and artists? Or is it because their psychology is so closely linked to the seat of God's pure creative force? Whatever the truth of this, there is no doubt that homosexuals have made solid contributions to the arts beyond their numbers.

It's clear by the long history of homosexuality and its acceptance by many cultures, and its adoption even by warrior cults such as the Spartans and the Macedonians that it is not in any way unnatural. In fact, many of the world's most important leaders such as Alexander the Great and perhaps Winston Churchill and Abraham Lincoln, had homosexual relationships – not to mention John Lennon! It is clearly a natural expression of the raw life force that resides in the first chakra, every bit as natural as the heterosexual behaviors that reside in the second chakra.

Homosexuality no doubt has even conferred evolutionary advantages. Remember, in social animals, it is not just the individual that is subject to natural selection, but the group and its gene pool. A group that is more cohesive with less internal conflict may be more likely to survive than a group with a higher amount of internal competition, say, for example, over mating privileges. In many social animals and in many primitive tribes, only the alpha male, or leader, is able to breed, and subordinate males generally accept this *status quo*. Of course, inevitably, challenges from young, strong males occur, and new alpha males arise, but if this process of challenge is too frequent, the group dynamic will not ever be stable for prolonged periods of time. However, if some of the non-alpha males lose their desire to breed, perhaps instead channeling their libido toward homosexual activity, they are not as likely to engage in conflict with the alpha male. They may also use homosexual behavior as an extension of mutual grooming activities to build and maintain a positive relationship with the alpha male or each other.

Reducing the risk of an envious male violently attacking the alpha male, possible killing him or leaving him injured and less likely to breed, is especially important in humans with their ability to use weapons. A less formidable male with a blunt or sharp object can ambush and defeat a much stronger opponent, so a mechanism to help non-breeding males to accept their status is even more important in humans than in any other social animal.

Since the alpha male is likely the repository of some of the best-adapted genetic traits in the group, by reducing risks to him, more offspring will carry those highly adaptive traits forward within the group's gene pool. The bottom line is that homosexual behavior clearly does confer distinct survival and adaptive advantages for the group, and by extension for the individuals in the group. Consequently, it should come as no great surprise that we find homosexual behavior in our closest evolutionary relative, the highly-sexual bonobo chimpanzees, for whom it appears to be a gesture of submission and an extension of mutual grooming behavior. This behavior would probably not be carried forward over countless generations as a universal aspect of the bonobos' group activities if it did not confer some evolutionary edge.

Now that we've pointed out some of the positive aspects of the first chakra, we can return to a discussion of some of its pitfalls. Does our culture chronicle any references to the potentially negative, Thanatos-linked aspects of the first chakra intelligence and its impact on the individual if it becomes an aberrant influence? The answer is certainly yes, within Greek mythology there is an interesting reference and parallel.

Most of us are familiar with the term "Pandora's Box." This is a story from Greek mythology about Pandora, a woman who opened a mythical, magical box and released a rush of evils. Pandora was the "Eve" of Greek mythology, the first woman, whose name means "all gifted" because all the Gods and Goddesses on Mount Olympus each bestowed her with a gift — although many were not positive. But Pandora is not known for the meaning of her name, but for opening that famous box that the Gods had given to her, and which carries her name to this day. When she opened Pandora's Box, it released "burdensome toil and sickness that brings death to men… diseases… and myriad other pains."

And so it is for those who open their own Pandora's Box by allowing the first chakra to explode into their behavioral and emotional world outside the channels of its natural expressions: its positive homosexual expression and functions. If this chakra runs wild, the effect can be much as the Greeks described with the opening of Pandora's Box. What we call perversions live here – in particular sadism, masochism and all the extensions of those behaviors up to and including the eroticization of death. With much of the life energy dissipated at this level, the body's bioenergetics and perhaps the immune system are weakened, letting the body play host to the aforementioned sickness, death, diseases and myriad other pains.

But how does someone open Pandora's Box? People do this by gravitating toward the pull of its behaviors, until, at a certain point a line is crossed and the behaviors seem to take over. It is a case of the dictum that we create our habits and then our habits create us. So, trifling and experimenting with the dark side of the powerful forces lurking "below" in the first chakra, no matter how innocent it may seem at first, such as the aforementioned teenagers cutting themselves with razor blades, can lead people into damaging and dangerous mental states from which it is very difficult to emerge.

For maximum positive spiritual development, much of the energies of the first and second chakras must be directed upward toward the higher chakras. This is why various monastic and religious practices advocate sexual abstinence, and notice that this has always included prohibition of heterosexual behavior as well as homosexual, the latter of which, ironically, is more possible to occur in sexually segregated monastic settings.

Sexual abstinence can be spiritually advantageous because the system of the chakras can be likened to a column of water, with a faucet at each chakra. If any of the faucets is opened too far, whether the first or the second one, or even the third, fourth or fifth, the water will not rise higher up the column. However, on the bright side, if any or even all of the faucets representing the "worldly" chakras are opened modestly and proportionally, there is still plenty of water to rise up the column, that is, plenty of energy to cascade upwards, fuel the higher chakras and enable emotional health as well as spiritual and religious growth and achievement.

9: THE ARCHITECTURE OF THE SPIRIT

Throughout recorded history the number seven has had profound significance within man's various belief systems. Having presented the idea that there are seven centers of consciousness in the human being, it is interesting to observe that the number seven appears frequently in various contexts within the world's religions and their scriptures. The concept of the chakras comes to us more openly from the Eastern religions, but the number seven is also very prominent in countless contexts within the western Faiths.

For example, in Judaism and Christianity the creation took seven days. The normal Jewish menorah has seven candles (only the special Hanukkah menorah has nine). In the Kabbalah system of Jewish mysticism, the Deity created the world with seven divine attributes which infuse throughout thc entire creation. In fact, the Bible uses the number seven many hundreds of times, much more than any other number. The number seven appears in the Book of Revelation alone 54 times including references to the seven seals, the seven churches, the seven spirits, the seven vials, the seven trumpets, the seven stars and several other "sevens." Other Christian references include the seven deadly sins, the seven heavenly virtues and the Seven Sacraments.

In Islam, Allah created seven heavens and seven earths. As in the Judeo-Christian tradition, He also created the seven days of the week. The creation of man required seven stages. Pilgrims to Mecca must circle the Kaaba seven times.

The number seven also appears in some very fundamental physical contexts. Seven is the number of colors in the spectrum of visible light: red, orange, yellow, green, blue, indigo and violet. It is also the number of notes in western music's major and minor musical scales. The eighth note in a scale is the same as the first only an octave higher, and the other notes of the scales are sharps and flats of the seven named notes, the specifics dependent on the scale being played.

In short, there is indeed something very special about this number, and it may now be clear that it is the reality that there are seven levels of consciousness that is the underpinning of many of these references.

We described in the previous chapter what these seven levels are, and how they ascend from the sacrum up the length of the spine and into the head. We also described how each center is associated with a unique energy, and how each one transforms the energy from the level below into a more refined form, then in turn passing that form upward through the spine where it is again refined to a higher form of consciousness. We've also noted that each chakra is associated with major cluster of physical nerves called a ganglion.

This passage of energy from one center to the next implies a structure connecting them, and indeed such a structure exists. Representations of it appear, and in a remarkably similar form, across myriad religions and in other cultural, and even medical, contexts.

The same Hindu traditions that introduced us to the seven centers of consciousness or chakras, also introduce us to the structure that connects and organizes them while providing the energetic axis of the human being. But let's first turn our focus to something more familiar and begin with what is certainly the most common representation of this structure in western culture.

The official symbol for the American Medical Association, and by extension much of western medicine, is the Staff of Aesculapius, a column with a single snake coiled around it. It is named after Aesculapius, the Greek god of medicine who was killed by a thunderbolt from Zeus for enabling too many people to live longer and thus reducing the number of people passing into the underworld.

The other symbol commonly associated with medicine and often confused with the Staff of Aesculapius is the Caduceus of Mercury. This is also a staff but has two serpents coiled around it, two wings toward the top, and at its crown a globe. What is most interesting about the caduceus is that the two coiled serpents have a form that is familiar to us now in a way that it could not possibly have been when it was introduced into medical symbolism near the turn of the century, let alone when the symbol arose over two-thousand years ago within Greek mythology. That form is the unmistakable shape of the double helix, which we now recognize as the structure of our DNA, the molecule that sits at the core of our genetic make-up. Is it a coincidence that this common symbol within our medical profession happens to be congruent with the geometry of one of the most fundamental levels of our being?

Has this basic form, a vertical staff surrounded by two entwined helixes or serpents, usually associated with wings toward the top, above that a sphere, appeared in other cultures as a frequent historical motif, and does it often appear with clear spiritual connotations? The answer is absolutely "yes."

In the Old Testament, God tells Moses to create a fiery, brass serpent on a pole. In John 3:14 the Bible says, "And as Moses lifted up the serpent in the wilderness, even so must the Son of Man be lifted up." This dovetails with the Hindu concept of raising the serpent energy as a key part of spiritual growth.

In Aztec mythology, we find a similar form in the feathered serpent Quetzalcoatl. Sumerian mythology includes the image of two serpents crossed back and forth around a rod. The Egyptian Pharaohs were often pictured with coiled serpents on their foreheads, representing the destination of the divine fire which sprung from the sacrum and rose upwards to the head.

But most telling is the aforementioned Hindu concept of the coiled serpent. This is an energy called the serpent power, or *Kundalini* in Sanskrit. It originates at the base of spine in the sacrum and from there rises up to the crown of the head. Learning to awaken, control, and fully activate this "serpent" energy, ultimately raising it to pierce the chakras in sequential order, then finally bringing it at full strength to the highest chakras is the mechanism that brings enlightenment or pure God consciousness in yoga. This literally represents God "grabbing" all the spiritual energy in the body in our ultimate gift to Him.

With that in mind, let's again quote John 3:14 which says, "And Moses lifted up the serpent in the wilderness, even so must the Son of man be lifted up." There could hardly be a more obvious reference to the near-culturally ubiquitous spiritual structure of the double helix, or "serpent" power, and the spiritual goal of "raising" it, so that it can more powerfully energize the centers of consciousness through which we connect with God.

Now we can visualize a rough map of the human spirit: An invisible structure composed of a central axis and surrounded by a double helix of energy that extends from the sacrum to the crown of the head. At each end, and at every crossing, and widest points of divergence is a different chakra that is responsible for infusing us with its level of consciousness and letting us experience its associated sensations, urges and behaviors. The chakras progressively refine the life energy as it ascends upwards through the caduceus. Finally, the more of this energy that reaches the "crown" chakra at the top of the head, the more consciousness the modem to God can transmit to Him. This greater level of God consciousness equals a greater gift of consciousness to God in furtherance of the Great Cycle of Creation.

Consciousness, or life force, can be preserved at every level, which is the point of common monastic practices such as celibacy, or the life force can be released at one of the lower chakras, possibly dramatically reducing the amount of life force available for transmutation by the chakras above the one discharging excessive amounts of its essence. This is the process of dissipation, which can often occur through excessive sexual activity at the first and/or second levels, or even by falling so deeply into materialism at the third level that there is little energy available for love, such as with Charles Dickens' character Ebenezer Scrooge. Life force can also be dissipated at the fourth and fifth levels through rampant, obsessive romanticism or by "wallowing" in excessive pity, whether for another or for oneself. But in a healthy person, the energy passes along the double helix from one chakra to another, creating the dynamic range of feelings that we experience, whether in our everyday lives, our focus shifting into sexual activity, or our engaging in religious practices.

If we have a large concentration of consciousness at any given chakra, letting that life force drop to a lower chakra releases a large amount of life force energy, much like an electron that drops from a higher quantum state to a lower state which releases a photon, the unit of light energy. We feel this energy as stimulation, pleasure or perhaps as "fun." For example, a person spending his hard-earned money, and the inner sense of achievement that this represents, who spends his third chakra wealth on habitual visits to a lap dancing club until his money, and inner wealth, that is his sense of self-worth, are both dissipated. Of course, he has enjoyed this and the release of life force energy as it drops from a higher "quantum" state to a lower one.

In fact, each of the lower five chakras has an "abuse" associated with it, and if this abuse is allowed to dominate behavior, spiritual growth will be impeded at that level. These abuses are perversion, sexual excess, greed, selfish romanticism, and maudlin pity. For those who have read the preceding material, there is no need to enumerate which chakra with which each is identified.

But what about the sixth chakra? Can there be an abuse associated with it? The answer is yes, and this is the greatest wrong of all. For if the full force of the life energy is brought up all the way to the sixth level, creating an extremely powerful consciousness, but is then hoarded there instead of being passed on to God, this makes someone a Lucifer or an anti-Christ. By stealing for themselves what should be God's, they become someone, or something, who willfully puts themselves, if not above God, at least apart from Him. Such a person would likely have a great deal of charisma, willfulness and seeming wisdom, perhaps using these qualities to become powerful in the secular or political world. We must all be aware that such an individual can arise, perhaps as did Hitler, and if so, such a Godless individual with nearly supreme will and high intelligence can do a great deal of harm.

10: GUIDED EVOLUTION AND THE LEVELS OF CONSCIOUSNESS

One of the most divisive issues, at least in American society, that sharply separates religious and secular thinking is the issue of Divine creation versus Darwinian evolution. This conflict has long been so bitter that it has created entrenched disagreement in many areas of society, in particular regarding how we educate our children, including the content of school text books.

Fundamentalist Creationists believe that God directly created the world as it is, including all existing life forms, literally as described in Genesis. They take this as an article of faith with no compromise possible. Other Creationists, with a more scientific bent, allow for a more allegorical interpretation of Genesis, but both may rightly agree and point out that the laws of thermodynamics argue strongly against Darwinian evolution. They maintain that the progressive increase in structure and reduction in randomness that evolution requires is against nature's drive toward entropy, in other words, evolution is impossible according to some of science's own fundamental principles. And this objection to evolution is not unreasonable. By what incredible process of accidental happenstance can a soup of molecules become a highly-structured living thing that only then can begin to acquire a mechanism to reproduce itself and evolve, and all the time fighting the laws of thermodynamics? As well as the clock, before entropy returns it to the primordial tide pool, like a castle made of sand washing back into the sea? Finally, after billions of chemical combinations that almost could be alive but weren't, one finally gains the ability to replicate, becomes alive, and is off to the races.

Then through an endless series of additional chemical and then genetic accidents, the living things grow into multi-cellular organisms, which transform into fish and reptiles that reproduce sexually instead of by cellular division, and on to dinosaurs, mammoths and humans. Along the way arise gills, livers, kidneys, spinal columns and skeletons, lungs, eyes, brains and everything else that life as we know it requires, and all this comes to be, through the process of accumulated happy accidents.

It's no wonder that creationists can feel very certain about the impossibility of life arising through the purely accidental mechanisms proposed by evolutionary theory. Instead, they attribute creation to intelligent design and look to the traditional religious explanations for its mechanisms, many believing literally the account in Genesis that certainly doesn't involve any evolution.

But in order to completely refute evolution, the creationists must deny, or at least try to reason away, the fossil record which is *strongly* suggestive of evolution. Some of their thinking becomes very contorted, such as blaming the existence of fossils on the work of the devil. But yet these same creationists believe that God created the entire world, so how can they imagine that the devil was able to create certain parts of it, such as the fossil record and/or the strata of rock where the fossils are found?

Those who believe in evolution, or Darwinists, for want of a better term, feel secure in their beliefs because of that fossil record and what it's indicated, but also because evolution can be observed to be continuing today. One example of this is when bacteria gradually gain immunity to antibiotics through the process of adaptive selection. But it's the fossil record that provides the most unassailable evidence for evolution. Although relying only on the hard body parts such as shells and skeletons that fossilize well, they can demonstrate a fairly continuous spectrum of life forms from the simple to the more complex, starting with unicellular organisms and continuing on through the more primitive invertebrate and then vertebrate forms and on to mammals, from which spring hominids, finally culminating in the emergence of modern man or *Homo sapiens*.

Indeed, there are powerful arguments that can be brought to bear by both sides of the debate. Even within the domain of science, there is divergence here. The laws of thermodynamics argue against evolution, the fossil record and its accompanying geology argue for it.

In some ways, based on observation and evidence, both the creationists' intelligent design and Darwinian evolution appear highly unlikely if not impossible. But are these two processes really mutually exclusive? Or is the only possible mechanism a hybrid of the two systems, in which the process of life's development is driven by a creative energy from God that works counter to entropy and toward structure, but which still uses genetic selection as a key tool in the evolution of life?

Some people believe in just such a hybrid called "guided evolution" that suggests that God's creative force and natural selection can work together. In guided evolution, God works as the Creator, but instead of all life forms bursting on the scene at once fully formed, God gradually builds life's complexity, starting with the simplest organisms as in a Darwinian scheme, and then progressively building on His work as He improves the simpler forms to develop the more complex. In this system, God drives the broad strokes of evolution, with natural selection leveraging God's direct interventions to fine tune species' adaptations to various changing conditions, such as shifts in climate, or in the case of bacteria, resistance to antibiotics.

Guided evolution eliminates the argument against Darwinian evolution posed by its blatant violation of the laws of thermodynamics, laws which hold in virtually every other situation. With the idea that an external force working counter to entropy is driving the process of evolution, the truism that matter tends to go from order toward randomness, and thus life should never have developed, is no longer valid. As to the existence of forces that work counter to entropy, let's remember the recent discovery of Dark Energy as an essential quality of the universe. On the cosmic scale, it counters the ultimate entropic force, gravity, so why not similar forces, perhaps closely related, that counter entropy at the biological level?

Sadly, Darwinians continue to reject even the reduced level of intervention posited by guided evolution. This is not necessarily because these scientists are atheistic, no doubt many are not. It is because they don't see the need for it, they think that their pet series of chemical and biological accidents is all that is required, and point to their cherished fossil record as if it proves that no Divine intervention was involved. Which, of course, the fossil record in no way proves. Indeed, the fossil record speaks not at all to the issue of life's causality, only to the history of its progress.

But if we want to explore the possibility of guided evolution, by what process would it occur? Is there anything that can give us a clue as to how life made the big leaps that it has, from chemicals in a tide pool, to amoebas and bacteria, to cold-blooded fish and reptiles, to warm-blooded mammals and birds, to those that seem to have emotional attachment for their young, and then to those that form cohesive social groups, to higher animals with clear if nascent cognitive and communications skills, and finally to hominids and modern man? Clearly there were a series of massive leaps between the major phyla, classes, orders, and families that comprise the family tree of life.

Within modern Darwinian theory, there are two proposed systems of evolution. One is called gradualism, and it is closer to the more generally familiar idea that organisms change a little bit at a time, but that they are always changing. The other idea, called interrupted equilibria, sees a very different process, and one that is perhaps more interesting for our purposes here. In this system, periods of very little or truly incremental change are "interrupted" by major, possibly very rapid and certainly very fundamental, changes in life forms. These sudden interruptions in genetic equilibrium don't have to be of truly huge magnitude such as the demise of the dinosaurs and the rise of the mammals, an interruption can be as simple as a species changing because a landslide has blocked their water source. Both of these systems are accepted by some within mainstream science based on the fossil record and other evidence, and if anything, interrupted equilibria, the more recent theory, is starting to find more favor.

This is interesting because interrupted equilibria seems to fit very well with the idea of guided evolution, and in particular with the approach that will be developed here in this chapter. We have already identified discrete levels of consciousness within a human being. Is it possible that it is those same discrete levels of consciousness, each a unique "energetic intelligence" all its own, and which are hierarchical in nature, could be the driving force behind guided evolution? Indeed, some of the chakras also seem to exist within "lower" life forms and drive behaviors in them that are nearly identical to our own, the most obvious of which are the behaviors associated with sexual reproduction or the nurturing of the young.

So as was discussed earlier, in much the same way as Dark Energy works in opposition to entropy by overcoming the force of gravity, a similarly counter-entropic force could impede or reverse the thermodynamic decay of life's structures. Could it be that God's energetic intelligences, all of which still are manifest within us as chakras, are in fact the counter-entropic forces that enabled and drove the incredibly complex organizational process that scientists call evolution? If so, could it be that each major leap in the evolutionary process, that is each instance of interrupted equilibria coincides with life forms sequentially receiving, or at least reaching a point in their development where they are able to tune into, the energy of the next higher chakra?

We know that the earliest organisms reproduced by cellular division only. Earlier we mentioned that the first chakra is connected to the reproductive method of these single celled organisms. According to science, single celled organisms were the first life forms to appear on Earth. Is it possible that in the "first day" of creation, God made available the raw life force of the first chakra energetic intelligence, enabling the emergence of life? Was it this energetic intelligence rather than random chance that drove the organization of amino acids and nucleotides in the chemical soup into the first most primitive life forms?

But these organisms did not yet utilize or manifest the energy of the second chakra which enables sexual polarization into male and female – let alone any of the higher chakras as will be discussed later. In other words, an amoeba does not have genitals or a solar plexus, nor does it have a heart, whether in the physiological or emotional sense. The fact that it has only one chakra may be why such creatures have no front or back but instead have radial symmetry, with only one center. If all this is true, then the first chakra is the gift of the first day of creation.

Later, the capacity for sexual reproduction appeared in simple invertebrate organisms and still later in vertebrates such as fish, amphibians and reptiles. This represented a very large, and very abrupt jump in complexity, and while it is hard to imagine how there might have been intermediary life forms between the asexual and the sexual, such transitional organisms do exist. They are single celled organisms that, while reproducing through cellular division, first exchange genetic material through a process called conjugation in which a tube extends from one organism to another, through which passes DNA, creating a new and unique genetic mix in a way that simple cellular division cannot.

It is interesting that even some of the earliest organisms that reproduce sexually exhibit behavior that is not all that different from our own, or to put it more accurately, we continue to manifest sexual behavior that is not all that different from theirs. Our culture sometimes recognizes this through our language, for example, a sexually obsessed man who practically lives at a singles bar might be called a lounge lizard. Is it also possible that the sexiness associated with net stockings harkens back to some primitive textural cues dating to our reptilian ancestors, among the first creatures to sexually reproduce that shared our basic torso and limbs form?

We can observe in ourselves and in "lower" animals, similar sexual behavior, and that the sex organs are physiology congruent, as is the consistent location of the genitals toward the lower end of the spine. Given these facts, it is not out of line to posit that the sexual energy of all creatures is rooted in second chakra structures within their energetic physiology? Is it possible that God drove this major jump in life's complexity and advancement by introducing for its usage the essence of the second chakra energetic intelligence, a force that persists today even in ourselves? Or did life just reach the point where it could tune into this energy which was "always there?" In other words, by God's making this higher organizational principal or energetic intelligence available, whether by releasing it afresh or by life reaching the point of being able to utilize it, did He "guide" evolution forward from asexual to sexual reproduction?

Clearly, not all organisms were able to utilize this new energetic gift, and single-celled and other simple asexual organisms continued to thrive and to evolve incrementally in response to their environments. But for the organisms that could tune into, and utilize, this energy, there was a great leap forward into sexual reproduction. It is as if the planet's life learned an entirely new way of functioning, and brought it to bear in what might be seen as a second stage of creation.

Once this energy came to be utilized by life, it drove a rapid increase in complexity, functionality, and in particular adaptability. This is because sexual reproduction allows much more rapid conventional Darwinian evolution. With organisms that reproduce asexually, aside from the few that use conjugation, only mutations can create new genetic types. But with sexual reproduction, any time two organisms' mate, an entirely new and unique genetic combination comes into being. This drove much more rapid development of new types, and although this process was jump-started by God's gift of the second chakra, the resulting sexual reproduction could then radically leverage God's creative process through rapid Darwinian selection.

Indeed, science currently believes that for the first three billion years that life existed, there were primarily single-celled, asexual life forms. Did it take that long for these life forms to become sophisticated enough to integrate and apply the second chakra energetic intelligence? Of course, once sexual reproduction entered the picture, the entire spectrum of life developed from shrimp to dinosaurs to saber-toothed tigers and on to humans in one-sixth the time, around five hundred million years, that life languished in unicellular stasis.

Then is the second chakra the driving force behind a second epoch of sexually reproducing life, or simply put, the gift of the second day of creation?

If that is so, we might expect the next big jump to be toward organisms that have life processes, characteristics and capabilities that might be suggested by the introduction of the third chakra organizational principal and energetic intelligence. This center, associated with the solar plexus, handles our bodies' energy processes from digestion to metabolism to the acquisition of resources. It should be the next organizational principal that God brings to bear in a chakra-based guided evolution scenario. And this is exactly what the fossil record suggests.

When God introduces, or life gains the ability to utilize, the energy that drives the third chakra, there is another abrupt jump forward, and life acquires the capacity for vastly superior and more efficient management of energy. This enables the far greater sophisticated metabolic system we call warm-bloodedness. With the gift of the third chakra energetic intelligence, warm blooded creatures such as birds and mammals arose — perhaps derived from warm blooded dinosaurs, and this was the third phase of guided evolution, or in Judeo-Christian terms, the third day of Creation.

Of course just as single chakra creatures such as amoebas and bacteria continued to slowly evolve, life-forms such as reptiles and fish continued on as two-chakra beings, remaining cold blooded but continuing to evolve incrementally to adapt to their changing habitats.

But for the warm-blooded creatures, God would soon be offering another gift, a new form of energetic intelligence that would move life another great step forward. This gift would result not so much in physiological change as in behavioral and emotional advancement, although there is one striking anatomical feature that would develop. Interestingly, this new gift would be available only to life forms that had integrated the third chakra energy that gave them warmth, not the two-chakra life that remained cold, let alone those with single cells and single chakras. This gift was of the fourth chakra, and it should come as no surprise that it is the gift of love.

It was probably not a long time on the geological scale between the third and fourth gifts. But with the advent of fourth chakra love, mammals and birds began to manifest some new behaviors, in particular they began to care for their young. And, they also began to care *about* their young.

Imagine a mother sea turtle laying hundreds or thousands of eggs, and then following her highly-evolved instincts to bury the eggs in the sand in just the right place, far enough from the shore so they won't be washed out by the tides, but still close enough so the hatchlings might make it to the water before predators can snatch them off the sand. Her behavior is clearly perfected to maximize her offspring's chances of survival. But that is it, there is no care or concern for the hatchlings, in fact the mother will be nowhere nearby when the little ones break out of their shells and begin to scramble toward the water, some of them hopefully to survive on their own.

Contrast this behavior with that of a mother bird, who warms her eggs with her own body heat, then feeds and cares for her young until they are far more ready to face the world than are the turtle hatchlings. Furthermore, the mother bird will fiercely defend her young, and will even risk her own life by playing decoy to distract predators away from them. For some, however, this might still be interpreted as purely instinctive behavior, more akin to the mother turtle burying her eggs in just the right spot than to a human mother running into a burning building to save her child.

Today, scientists believe that birds are closely related to reptiles, perhaps even direct descendants of dinosaurs. It has been said that some of the dinosaurs were warm blooded and perhaps even cared for their young. If so, that merely means that they were still walking the Earth when God gifted the third and fourth chakras. There is no reason to insist that only birds and mammals could know warmth and love. Perhaps some dinosaurs rose to that level of sophistication by integrating the energies of the higher chakras, if so that capability may have been passed directly on to the birds. Of course, there is no way to easily prove that extended nurturing and willingness for self-sacrifice in birds has anything to do with love or emotions. But it does seem believable and in tune with common sense that these behaviors are somehow higher than those of the mother turtle. In any event, the possibility is certainly there, as is the appearance that it is so.

Perhaps the emotional nature of this evolutionary leap will be easier to accept in the case of our fellow mammals. When we see a mother dog licking its babies clean or playing with them, we can more easily resonate with her feelings of motherhood as they seem to be so similar to those in our own species. We also see in mammals an obvious anatomical distinction that we share with them, a distinction that further separates them and us from the fish and reptiles, and even the birds. This of course is the existence of the mammary glands from which mammals get their name. Mammary glands are a self-evident physical manifestation of the nurturing energy, and they could possibly not have come into being without the extended close contact between mothers and young that may have predated their full development.

The period of protection and close contact between mother and offspring can, in some cases, last for several or even many years. During this time the mother nurses and nurtures the babies, trains them as they grow into older cubs, kittens or pups, and finally challenges them as adolescents, evoking and stimulating more mature behavior patterns resulting in their striking out on their own. Naturally, all of this behavior applies to human mothers and children since, in spite of our bigger brains, we're still mammals who share the identical fourth chakra gift with the others. However we regard birds, it's very hard to argue that the mammalian mother has no feelings for her babies. In any event, one certainly wouldn't want to argue the case with a protective mother bear!

Fourth chakra love may have appeared first in the nurture of the young, but it has clearly taken on much more complex forms for us, and perhaps for other species in the development of pair and group bonding. While fish form massive schools that exhibit incredible coordination in their group motions, and also swarm during spawning, few would confuse these instinctive organizations with social groups where individuals form close bonds and complex hierarchical relationships with each other. These sophisticated forms of social organization arose not among the fish and reptiles, but later among the warm-blooded creatures. It is very evident today, as many living species of mammals are highly social with strong group bonds, and what appears to be an emotional connection between group members. For example, there is clear evidence of caring for the sick or injured among some of the higher mammals from elephants to lions, as well as what appears to be extended grieving for animals that have died. This behavior of animals grieving for their dead is quite well-documented, especially among elephants.

Does this all mean that these higher animals experience the same feelings of love as we do? Can animals that form lifelong mating pairs feel something akin to our romantic love? The answer could be yes, as one of the functions of all the feelings emanating from the chakras is to spur behavior. Consequently, it is easy to imagine that emotional cues and behavioral mechanisms that are very similar to those we experience exist within animals. The emergence of love within life forms poses an interesting question that challenges a strictly Darwinian interpretation of life's development. A characteristic like love, so clearly a spiritual quality, and so profound in the depth of its feelings for us and perhaps animals, is more obviously a Divine gift than is sexuality or warm-bloodedness and must stand as one of the most powerful arguments for Divine creation through guided evolution by successive causality via the attributes of the chakras.

If all this is true, the feelings of love that come with the fourth chakra are the gift God gave to life on the fourth day of creation.

If our chakra-based theory of guided evolution is to remain consistent, the next energetic intelligence to manifest in life would be the gift of communication, empathy and perhaps even compassion. Many mammals use characteristic vocalizations to attract partners for mating, to warn of predators, to intimidate prey, to warn off rivals and in general to communicate with those of their own species. Cats and dogs clearly communicate with their human companions. The question becomes at what point do these vocalizations go beyond instinctive behavior and reach the threshold of a more sentient form of communication? Part of the answer is that instinctive vocalizations might be identified because they are always the same. For example, danger or fear triggers an automatic set of behaviors in many animals, including warning vocalizations. These do not involve or require conscious choices; the vocalization is automatic and instinctive. Another example might be the songs of birds, which are often used to attract mates. With some exceptions, all members of a given bird species will vocalize the exact, identical birdsong. These songs are so consistently predictable that ornithologists in the field can use these calls to identify the species of a bird.

Clearly, among humans, vocalizations and communication can involve a sophisticated level of conscious choice, extending all the way up to singing, literature, poetry and oratory. This range of behavior is so distinct from a bird species using only a fixed vocalization that the distinction is self-evident. Of course, this does not mean that humans never use instinctive vocalizations. For example, when hurt or frightened, we scream, and this scream is not that different from the scream of a non-human primate or other animal that is experiencing similar danger or fear. But unlike "lower" animals, our ability to communicate is not limited to these instinctive calls.

This raises a question as we explore chakra-based guided evolution. Are there animals that arose prior to human beings that were, and are, able to use this fifth chakra energetic intelligence for consciously controlled communication? It does appear so, as primates, dolphins and many other animals do seem to exhibit more complex, unique and specific communications. For example, whales and dolphins seem to have a sort of language through which they communicate information that helps them to coordinate their activities, such as complex hunting and feeding behaviors.

But what about other elements of fifth chakra behavior, such as empathy and compassion? In her book *The Compassion of Animals, True Stories of Animal Courage and Kindness* author Kristin von Kreisler maintains that the answer is a resounding "yes." She offers numerous examples that she believes confirm her premise that animals are capable of this higher emotion. And she is not alone in that evaluation of her material. Paul G. Irwin, past president of the Humane Society of the United States, had this to say about her book and the position it takes:

> Through dozens of inspiring true stories, Kristin von Kreisler makes the case for a 'controversial' premise — that animals demonstrate genuine acts of compassion towards others every day. This book will remove the 'controversial' from that premise. Furthermore, her 16th chapter is entitled "Favors to Strangers."

The examples in this chapter indicate that the basis of some animal behavior is not dependent on fourth chakra love and its link to possessory relationships. If animals can exhibit kindness to strangers, then that is a classic indication of fifth chakra compassionate behavior.

If all this is true, and as we've shown there are indications that it is, then we humans may have inherited the potential for compassion from life forms that had already tuned into the fifth chakra energetic intelligence. Did "lower" animals actually precede us in the development of capacities that we generally regard as unique to our own species, such as compassion? Of course, if so, these were life forms that had already integrated the second, third and fourth chakra energetic intelligences into their psychology and behavior, and finally had also integrated the fifth chakra energetic intelligence as well.

So God gifted life forms with the ability to truly communicate with each other and to feel compassion for other living things at a certain point in the process of guided evolution, and that point was what Judeo-Christians might call the fifth day of creation.

So now we have taken the process of guided evolution from the amoeba to some of the higher mammals, with each major leap forward powered and guided by a new energetic intelligence, each of which is the essence of one of the chakras. If our system is to remain consistent, we should now see the emergence of the sixth chakra energetic intelligence in life.

The name of our species, *Homo sapiens* is Latin for "wise (or rational) man" and we are the only extant species of the primate family *Hominidae*. According to many scientists, *Homo sapiens* and our "Neanderthal" cousins *Homo sapiens neanderthalensis* both descended from a more primitive ancestor called *Homo heidelbergensis*. As *Homo sapiens*, we clearly now have the ability to utilize the sixth chakra energetic intelligence. The question is at just what point in hominid evolution did we gain this ability? That point in time is crucial because it can be said that it would mark our emergence as human beings.

While there are many other animals that appear to have many of the characteristics of the first five chakras, there is no other species besides ours that has tempted taxonomists to include the term "wise" in their species name. This is because humans do indeed have qualities that set them apart from all other living things, in particular a sense of right and wrong. This ability to discern right actions, in short, wisdom, is one the very qualities that we associate with our sixth chakras.

Animals will always act out the strongest signal that comes to them from among the chakras. This might be fight or flight, a sexual urge, the drive to dominate a social group, the desire to nurture and protect young, or even perhaps the emotion to grieve for the dead or to help another being. There is no editing applied to these impulses because there is nothing to edit them, there is no seat of wisdom. But in humans, the sixth chakra has the wisdom to evaluate and prioritize the incoming urges from the other chakras, resulting in behavior that is not simply determined by which urge is the most compelling, but by what action is correct – even morally correct. It is this unique energetic intelligence, or at least its strong presence in us, that sets us apart from all other life forms on Earth.

The sixth chakra in humans manifests so many characteristics that set us apart from other life forms that it is hard to decide where to start enumerating them. It is the seat of our interest in learning and philosophy, the home of our religious inclinations, the arbiter of our morality, the inner courtroom for our sense of justice, the locus of our capacity to appreciate music, art and beauty, and it is conductor of the orchestra of all our faculties, drives, desires and sensibilities. Taken in aggregate, these abilities that live in our sixth chakra set us worlds apart from any other life form and signify that with the advent of man, the final step in the process of guided evolution came to fruition. Whatever our flaws, and they are myriad, because we have a strongly functional sixth chakra, we are literally the crown of creation.

How long did it take for early hominids to begin manifesting sixth chakra characteristics? It's likely that this capacity, once the organism acquired the ability to tune into it, or once it was introduced by God, first began to manifest in earlier hominid species. But once the spark was there, the energetic intelligence drove and directed the chakra's more sophisticated implementation through further stages of hominid development in a fairly rapid burst, characteristic of the interrupted equilibria mode of evolution.

It's very likely that Neanderthals, for example, who drew cave paintings and buried their dead, had a sixth chakra energetic implementation that was somewhat like our own, but perhaps less refined. Just because this energetic intelligence sets us apart from all pre-human living creatures, there is no reason to believe that at least some of the more advanced hominids did not have sixth chakra characteristics and behaviors, whether well-developed or rudimentary. In fact, without this energetic intelligence, these earlier hominids and primitive humans may not have had the social stability to provide a basis for the development of modern man.

The gift of sixth chakra energetic intelligence was God's final creative act to complete the chain of life on Earth, and after this sixth day, there was no more guided evolution and then, as Genesis tells us, God rested on the seventh day. Since then, God has not introduced any additional chakras or type of energetic intelligence, but it must be remembered that all the previous chakras remain active in the life forms that utilize some or all of them, and it is these energetic intelligences that continue to sustain life and counter entropy.

With God resting, evolution has proceeded on a strictly Darwinian basis as we observe today. Sadly, because scientists can observe evolution continuing today on the basis of Darwinian natural selection, they leap to the incorrect assumption that this is how it has always been. But scientists do have a recent model demonstrating how life can develop with intelligent guidance. In fact, life's natural development has lately been augmented by a new form of guided evolution, this time not from the intelligence of God but from the intelligence of man. This started with selective breeding, which created the different breeds of dogs and other animals, and the hybridization of plants which vastly increased crop yields. But now man has gone well past these relatively natural processes and into gene splicing, genetic engineering and even the creation of entirely synthetic DNA.

Does synthetic DNA mean the creation of life by man that is outside of God's own creative process? The answer is no, because no mix of chemicals, including synthetic DNA, can be truly alive without the ability to tune into one or more of God's gifts of energetic intelligence. This ability is probably a function of the double helix of DNA resonating with the double helix of energetic life, as represented by the Caduceus of Mercury and the Kundalini. In short, if one bag of chemicals that happens to have a long natural history can tune into God's energetic intelligence, why can't another bag of chemicals that man assembled precisely to closely emulate those naturally able to tune in? In either case, the real "life" comes from tuning in to God and His energetic intelligence, not from a pond, or a test tube, of amino acids. When man creates life forms that do not require DNA, and thus do not resonate with the caduceus, maybe then he will be truly generating fully synthetic life. Until then, man is just crudely reverse engineering God's work.

Like so many other energies, the life forces appear to exhibit quantum characteristics, that is to say that these energies differ from each other only in discrete steps, with no intermediate levels. This should come as no surprise, since it is quantum theory that first recognized that an observer, which is to say consciousness, affects the quantum state of subatomic particles and photons. It isn't surprising to see this emerging congruence between the deep functions of physical energy and those of the life energies.

So now we have seen how God used six of the chakras to guide evolution from the amoeba to *Homo sapiens*. But haven't we forgotten something? What about the seventh chakra? Is that as unique to man as is the sixth chakra? Why have we not included it as one of God's gifts that drove creation?

The answer is that the seventh chakra is an entirely different type of energetic center. It is much more an extension of God *into* a life form than it is a quality of the life form itself. It is God's tendril into an amoeba, by which He derives whatever small amount of Dark Energy that the amoeba can generate, and it is God's broadband connection to a human, enabling the wholesale transfer of our much greater consciousness bandwidth. Of course, this is a two-way connection that enables a human with a functioning sixth chakra to look upward and experience God. This upward look toward God is not something that the lower animals can do, since it is a capability of the sixth chakra, and animals do not have much, if any, sixth chakra energetic intelligence.

But it underscores the truth of Christianity when it says there is only one way to God, through Christ, because when the followers of Jesus say Christ, whether they know it or not, they are talking about the sixth chakra, the gift that God gave us on the sixth day of creation and the culmination of the long process of Him making man from dust.

11: WHY DOES GOD LET BAD THINGS HAPPEN?

As we examine Genesis, we see that in spite of exhausting Himself to the point where He needed to rest, God also saw that what He made was good. This indicates that God remained at that time as a Witness, consciously experiencing, and already judging, the universe He created. He may have been down, but He was not out.

Also notice that Genesis makes no mention of an eighth day. It does not say "on the eighth day God began to take complete control over all creation." Remember that if you believe God created our world, you must believe that God created the entire Universe, something incomprehensibly vast, including billions of galaxies the size of our own Milky Way or the nearby Andromeda, and each of those in turn containing billions of stars and planets, literally trillions upon quadrillions of worlds. Although God's consciousness extends throughout this entire creation, He clearly does not exert close control over every event that occurs in the universe. Indeed, He clearly allows the laws of physics to hold sway over the goings on of matter and energy from subatomic particles to solar systems, and has delegated the life energies to creatures from amoebas to monkeys and free will among us humans to exercise much of the conscious influence and control that is evident in the domain of life.

So, in our era, God, having thus delegated control over events, is still resting, still reconstituting Himself after the incredible Act of Creation that He performed over those first six days or epochs. As we've discussed up to now, around 70% of the universe has become, or has reverted to existing as, Dark Energy. This means that the majority of whatever portion of God's essence He converted to matter and energy at the creation has been returned to Him. Of course, this has taken, according to today's astrophysicists, around 14 billion years. So even though the process is ongoing, it will likely be hundreds of millions or even billions of years before God has been restored to a significantly greater extent than He has been so far, so He will not likely take a much greater role in shepherding human events for a very long time. That means that for the foreseeable future, we won't be able to blame God for "bad" things that happen significantly more than we can now.

Since He is still resting, at least to some extent, the Universe including of course, our planet, is subject to the events and effects caused by the millions, likely trillions or quadrillions, of free wills that have arisen as part of God's creation, including our own. It is also subject to the effects of the mechanical cause-and-effect processes operating according to the laws of physics since the creation.

Furthermore, the universe is apparently subject to random or chaotic processes and events that also spring from the chaotic Big Bang that marked God's initial creation. This includes on the grand scale stars being born and dying, planets such as ours coming into their fruition, and billions of years later, being destroyed in cataclysms such as super novae. It includes disease causing organisms coming into being and causing rampant suffering and death, and it includes some organisms of the infected species, such as humans, surviving such a plague and living on. And it also includes tragedies on the personal level, tragedies that affect us humans in our daily lives. Many events are determined by a combination of all these factors, including human free will, which together can cause an event that is certainly not the intent of the humans involved, nor of God.

Let's examine such an event, fictional, but similar to many that may have actually happened. Let's imagine, in this case, an event in which a school bus driver gets drowsy, goes to sleep at the wheel, and drives off a cliff, causing death and injury to dozens of innocent children. Events such as this have happened, and even to innocent children, perhaps even to children who should, by some ways of thinking, be protected by an all-controlling God because they are attending parochial schools.

At this point this author must insert a thought about a recent development near his residence. A church school bus carrying dozens of children collided with another vehicle and went over an embankment. The driver was killed, and over 20 children were injured, some critically. The fictional story here was written months before this accident occurred, so obviously this story is in no way based on, related to, or inspired by this particular accident. There was no indication that the accident was caused by anything but bad weather, and there was no finger pointed at the bus driver who, in any event, had been killed. But that having been said, it does illustrate the point here, that even children on a church school bus can be involved in a terrible accident that is certainly not any fault of their own. Nor is it the result of any fault of God. It was a random accident caused by the even greater randomness of the world's chaotic weather patterns.

Some say events similar to our fictional story are all part of God's plan or His will. They are not, they happen because God does not control everything that occurs. And it is certainly not for us to judge God by saying that He has willed or planned such things. He has created an almost infinite Universe after which He began resting by necessity, so He is not currently overseeing every event in every corner of His creation. And even though He may "see" something if His attention is somehow drawn to it, He has left many events to random physical processes and much of the ability to consciously influence His creation to the autonomous free wills that inhabit it, such as ours, including our imagined bus driver.

Now let's take a closer look at our *fictional* tragic school bus accident. To start the chain of events, the school bus driver stayed up until 3:00 am drinking alcohol the night before, because an old college friend happened to drop by, and staying up drinking was what they'd always done together. So, when the driver's alarm clock woke him up at 7:00 am, he clearly had not had enough sleep, but got up anyway only to discover that he had a bad hangover. Had he not had a couple of strong cups of coffee, he might not have felt good enough to go to work, but he did drink the coffee so he went to work instead of calling in sick.

Because he didn't call in sick but did go to work, he ended up driving his older model school bus when he was in no shape to do so. Now let's imagine the condition of that old school bus. It so happened that it had a small exhaust leak, unnoticeable normally, that happened to add incremental levels of carbon monoxide to the air within the bus. This level of carbon monoxide contamination was not enough to put an alert driver to sleep, but just enough to sedate our already drowsy driver, helping to make him doze off.

In total, had his life not been misdirected by the random event of a friend dropping by, and had this random event not triggered a cascade of bad decisions, and had not the bus had the exhaust leak that contributed to the driver's drowsiness, the dead and injured children would still be alive, healthy and happy. It was not God's will or part of God's plan that this bus driver should have a drop in friend, stay up late drinking, then choose other wrong actions, and the exhaust leak may have not been noticed by human observers because it was so slight, nor by God within the immensity of the universe. None of this can be blamed on God. Nor were these events and their tragic consequences something the children or their loved ones would have in any way deserved. Events such as this are just things that can and do happen in a world that God does not micromanage.

As tragic as such an accident might be, it pales in comparison to the death and suffering caused by wars. World War II alone brought the deaths of tens of millions of human beings, as did World War I. If there is ever a World War III, those numbers will be eclipsed by an order of magnitude or worse with hundreds of millions, or even billions, of people being killed and most of the rest of the world's population facing horrendous suffering. The amazing thing about war is that unlike natural disasters, they are the general result of the misuse of the human will, and the misdirection of human intelligence.

But many religious people believe that God is all powerful, omniscient, and that everything that happens is somehow part of His plan. Does this really make sense? How can the terrible things that are common to life such as war not only happen, but happen frequently? And how can suffering and death ultimately come to all of us and to all our loved ones? Is God cruel? No, again, God is resting, He has given us literally the entire creation of the Universe in all its richness, and that is plenty. He cannot closely control every event in the nearly infinite universe that He created. Will God ever stop resting and bring an era of pure happiness and love, with no accidents, no war, no cruelty, even no disease?

The fact is, God does grow stronger every minute, but very, very slowly. He does become more capable of Divine intervention with every passing second because consciousness is constantly returning to Him from all the life in the universe, making Him progressively more capable of such intervention. But as we discussed earlier, it has taken over 14 billion years for God to reach the strength and ability to intervene that He has now, so a meaningful change is likely quite far off. But on the other hand, like many gradual processes, this one may be subject to a tipping point, that is a point in God's regeneration when there might be a quantum leap in His interventionary power, and He may be able to, or choose to, take a more active role at a more detailed level. But unless such a tipping point is reached, or until God chooses to stop resting and we enter the eighth day, we will remain subject to the effects of bad human choices from negligence to thievery to world wars. We will also be straws in the winds of destructive "random" processes such as tornados, tsunamis and hurricanes, as well as the inexorable consequences of aspects of the creation such as solar cycles and the slow but certain tectonic processes that frequently result in volcanoes and earthquakes.

But saying that God is not determining all events is not to say that the prayer of a righteous man is not without effect. Remember, God looked at His creation and found it good, and is still looking, still listening, and God has the power to do absolutely anything He wills, including answering a prayer that touches Him. God loves us beyond all our imaginations, the closest we can come to imagining His love is to know our love for our own children, and He may hear our fervent, righteous prayers and use His hand to fulfill them if He so chooses.

Why does God answer prayers but not automatically stop horrible natural disasters and the actions of evil people? The answer to this question and the apparent disparity it takes into account brings us to the root of how God relates and interacts with His creation. The disparity between His response to prayer and his evident tendency to ignore natural forces and even evil people is due to His increased receptivity to higher levels of consciousness. Even for an everyday person who is praying sincerely, let alone for a highly-evolved spiritual being, a “saint” or a holy man, the prayers are, by their very nature, being formed within a person’s higher levels of consciousness.

It is information emanating from these higher levels of consciousness to which God is the closest and has the most receptivity.

This can be contrasted with the much lower levels of consciousness that drive the actions of evil people which do not have upper chakra activity and thus are not on God's radar. So what happens when righteous people, with established connections to God through their higher levels of consciousness, are praying fervently for God to change the behavior of evil people? This brings us to a discussion of the Jewish Holocaust, perhaps the greatest example of Divine inaction in the face of righteous prayer in recent experience.

There can be no doubt, that if God hears any prayers, He heard the prayers of His chosen people as they faced the most heart-rending terrors and horrors that any people have faced. Why did God not soften the hearts of the Nazis or worked through the actions of good people to save these millions of innocents? Of course, it must be said that there are numerous anecdotal incidents where individual free wills chose positive actions during the Holocaust, sometimes in the face of grave personal danger. Schindler is an example, as is the less well known work of Dr. Felix Kersten, who manipulated Heinrich Himmler to release many thousands of concentration camp prisoners. But certainly, on the grand scale, God did not intervene and millions suffered and perished in spite of their prayers. Why could God not influence the evil people who willed the atrocities of the Holocaust? This is because the evil choices and actions of these people could never have originated within the higher levels of consciousness with which God is most connected. It is true that the higher levels of consciousness in these people could have been awakened, but that would have required their desire to do so, not at all in evidence, their own effort to change which was not forthcoming, and a great deal of time spent in spiritual growth which they did not spend. While like all people, they potentially could have awakened the centers through which God could most readily influence them, they did not. And if these levels are not awakened, then the qualities of mercy, compassion, love and conscience that would have to become active to reverse the heartless, merciless and mindless choices leading to the Holocaust, would not be significant voices in the decision-making processes of these evil people. So, tragically, all the events that occurred in the Holocaust were left to the free wills of the Nazis.

But, in the face of the prayers of millions of righteous people, why would not God intervene directly and guide these evil people to reverse their beyond-evil actions? The answer goes again to the fact that the upper levels of consciousness are not only the seats of good choices, they are also our connections to God. So, if these evil peoples' upper levels of consciousness are relatively inactive and not awakened, God's voice, raised in response to the prayers of the good, will still be very, very quiet and dim to the Nazis. He couldn't influence them because they could not hear Him.

So, since God's voice will have little influence on them, their free will choices will be most strongly influenced by the tendencies, forces and voices, both from within and without, that speak to them through their own lower levels of consciousness. Consequently, these peoples' actions will be motivated primarily by these influences, which drive behaviors motivated by fear, aggressive instincts, the urge for conquest, territoriality, possessiveness, acquisitiveness and simple greed, as well as plain old lust for power. And since these behaviors arise from of the predominance of the lower levels of consciousness, they will not be mitigated by the higher emotions since these can come only from the higher centers, which are not strongly activated in these evil people.

But in spite of the fact that God does not generally overrule the free wills of human beings, probably having even less ability to influence the evil than the good, He has instilled in all of us the capacity for enlightened, humane behavior. But He has left the utilization of that capacity up to us, with very mixed results.

If Hitler chooses to do evil, it is not part of God's methodology to stop him through His own direct, miraculous, if you will, actions. But note that the task of stopping Hitler was indeed carried out, and that it was carried out by people who did have the ability to hear their higher centers and thus to listen to God. Unfortunately, even with these peoples' highly-evolved morality and correct motivation, the result of their actions was World War II, with much additional suffering and loss of life resulting from their actions, but all necessary for good men to eliminate the problem of Hitler.

As for natural disasters, there is either no consciousness involved at all or only the most rudimentary, lowest level form that may occur in inanimate matter. So, natural disasters, especially as they are in process and have not yet caused loss of life, do not make a serious blip on God's radar screen either. Such natural, quasi-random processes have been happening since the Big Bang and God has *not* been guiding every atom or molecule as the universe has formed and continued on in its physics-driven, and random, processes.

Nonetheless, we are God's eyes and spies as to what is going on in our little piece of the universe, and our prayers are one way that God gets this information. Through our observations, and especially our prayers, we can perhaps help to focus God's attention on things of seeming importance to us, and hopefully sometimes to Him.

So even if God does not notice the random workings of inanimate objects, and does not tune in readily on, or easily influence, human machinations emanating from the lower levels of consciousness, it is not because He does not hear the fervent prayers of millions of righteous people. That He does not answer every prayer is not an indictment of God, rather it is immutable evidence that He has delegated much of what happens here to our free wills rather than micro- or even macro-managing events among us human beings. What He has done for us is to provide scriptural and religious guidance that offers everyone the opportunity to become righteous and to make righteous choices. That is a tremendous gift, but our choice to accept or reject it is up to free wills, not up to Him.

So clearly, many prayers remain unanswered, even prayers offered by righteous people for the best causes. But it is not because these fail to command God's attention and is not because God willfully picks and chooses who to favor with answered prayers. It is because we are still in the seventh day, and God is still resting. So perhaps the best answer to the riddle of why a just God allows bad things to happen to good people, might be that God simply does the best He can, and we are not fit to accuse Him of doing anything less than His best. Sadly, the simple truth is that while God can do anything, He cannot do everything.

12: HOW RELIGIONS WORK AND HOW THEY CAN WORK TOGETHER

It might be hard to accept that virtually any religion can bring someone to God. The religion can even have doctrines that are obviously untrue. The religion can advocate behaviors that are socially damaging, including Jihadist actions that seem patently unholy to non-Muslims and to many mainstream Muslims as well. But yet even the most violent Jihadist, or even a suicidal member of a cult like Heaven's Gate or People's Temple, can legitimately find God through religious experiences engendered by their faith, its errors notwithstanding. How can this be?

It is because God does not come to us, He is always with everyone, and in fact we cannot escape His presence, only ignore or deny it. It is we who must come to God, and this does not happen because of the correctness or social value of our beliefs and doctrines, but rather in spite of them. We can only come to God when we judge ourselves worthy of facing Him, and then feel confident of His acceptance when we choose to open the inner door to the Divine Presence. This is usually accomplished when an individual feels that they have followed the strictures of their faith, and thus have proven to themselves that they are worthy of coming together with God. Every religion has a set of requirements that must be followed or achieved to make an individual feel worthy. Fulfilling these requirements can be viewed as a rite of passage that, when achieved, enables feelings of worthiness that allow a person to open their own inner door to God.

Simply put, all religions work by providing their own unique rite of passage that someone can come to believe they've performed correctly. This is not a rite of passage from childhood to adolescence or from adolescence to adulthood. This is a rite of passage from feelings of unworthiness to feelings of worthiness. By achieving success in performing this rite of passage, people come to judge themselves worthy enough to open up to God. It is simply by achieving their religion's rite of passage, and *not* because they happen to believe (or not believe) in their religion's cosmology, creation stories and accounts of miracles, that they can get out of their own way and turn to God who is, after all, always waiting within.

The key is that people need only perform their religion's rite of passage to *their own* satisfaction, not to anyone else's, or even to God's, to enable their turning toward the Creator. This is because each person has the power to be the *de facto* judge of their own worthiness, since they alone can choose to step through their own inner door to the Divine. Of course, they are also the only ones whose feelings of unworthiness can keep that door closed. And there is no self-deception here, only what the person truly believes matters, not what they may try to tell themselves.

God is always there inside, we couldn't escape Him if we tried, we just have to make ourselves feel worthy of His presence so we can sincerely make the choice to turn to Him, and He can be experienced instantly. Giving us a path to those feelings of worthiness, and thus to God, is the true function of all religions. The truth or falsehood of the religion's doctrines, scriptures, mythologies and God-name is completely extraneous and irrelevant to this process.

Because we are the judges of our own worthiness, almost any religion can help us to find God, because to work, a religion must be believed and practiced, and that is all. It does not have to be perfect or superior to others. It does not have to be the One True Faith. If an individual believes in any given religion, then, by extension, the individual believes in the validity of its core rite of passage. They certainly don't call it a rite of passage, and they perhaps don't even know what the term "rite of passage" means, but when they jump through the hoops held out for them by their faith to their own satisfaction, the resulting feelings of worthiness can trigger a genuine religious experience that can include a sense of contact with God.

This is what makes cults and other bizarre fringe sects so dangerous. Even if the leader of the cult is a fraud, and all its "scriptures" complete fiction, if someone comes to believe in it and sincerely believes that they have met its standards, in other words that they've performed its rite of passage, then they can gain the feelings of worthiness they need to open their inner door to God. The truth of the "religion" is absolutely irrelevant. Belief in it, belief in its rite of passage, and belief that its requirements have been met can bring feelings of worthiness that can open the door to a religious experience that is authentic, even if the religion that enabled it is far from that.

And thus, insincere or mistaken religions or teachers can sometimes be as effective in bringing people to God as those that are "true," whatever that means. While this is a problem as it can bring people under the control of false prophets and charlatans such as crooked televangelists, fortunately there can also be a silver lining. While such a connection to God will perhaps result in the creation of a true believer in a false religion, the on-going effects of the opening to God's presence can still be transformative in a positive way, even for people in the most abusive cult. No matter the context, God's influence can generate benefits for such individuals, their families, and society. God’s influence may even guide the individual out of the cult.

The idea that religious experiences are enabled by performing a rite of passage that leads to feelings of worthiness rather than belonging to the “one true church” explains much. It explains how people become fervent believers in literally hundreds of Christian denominations or sects, with many of these organizations claiming to be the only one that is correct and judging the others as false or even Satanic. These people are not pretending about the religious experiences they receive, which can all be genuine whether people are Baptists, Jehovah's Witnesses, Seventh Day Adventists, Presbyterians, Mormons, Catholics or Muslims. It doesn't matter if someone attends the Crystal Cathedral or a small corner church in the ghetto, God is waiting inside each believer, there for all. Church doctrine and the details of ritual are virtually irrelevant, provided they can engender feelings of worthiness that enable the believer to open the inner door to God, who is there waiting.

Doctrines, dogmas and specific rituals are relevant only in that an adherent can believe in them and follow them. The particulars can vary over a wide spectrum. For example, some Christian denominations speak in tongues, others say that speaking in tongues is prohibited and of the devil. Christians holding either of these completely contradictory beliefs are equally likely to have an authentic religious experience. It makes little difference exactly what you believe as long as you believe in God, come to believe that you have become worthy of Him, and act in a positive way on those beliefs to open the inner door.

Just as with Christian denominations, it doesn't matter if, by circumstances of birth, a Muslim happens to be a Sunni or Shiite. It doesn't matter if a Jewish person is Orthodox or Reform. It doesn't matter if you call the Creator God, Allah, or Yahweh. It doesn't matter if a believer is a Native American who calls God the Great Spirit. It only matters that a person comes to feel worthy of being in God's presence and opens the door inside. If that has happened, that person finds God and his or her religion and its rite of passage have served their purpose.

Later we will examine in detail the unique rites of passage that the major religions utilize. All are different, and although all can be equally effective in bringing feelings of worthiness, some are much more difficult than others. An easier rite of passage, such as submission to God, can be quite effective and result in a very rapidly spreading religion as is Islam. Difficult rites of passage can mean that a faith spreads more slowly, such as Judaism. But whether a rite of passage is easy or difficult, people can backslide from their practices, lose their feelings of worthiness and perhaps even feel that they've lost their connection to God. But the reversal cannot be complete, once they've found God, they are forever different, because they *know* God is there from personal experience, and they should know that they can come closer to Him again by abandoning whatever they are doing or thinking that has made them feel unworthy.

But just finding God is not the entire process. Once established, our relationships to God can be deepened and developed. As we come closer to God, we begin to have a sharper sense of what God wants, we may even "feel" a rebuke from Him from time to time for something we do, say, or even think. Building our relationship with God can become our main purpose in life, but this does not happen to the detriment of our other positive goals, in fact quite the contrary, it accrues to their betterment.

The way religions can work to help us with further spiritual growth can be introduced by a phrase that Jesus used to confront His disciples and believers. He addressed them as "ye of little faith" and by saying this, introduced the idea that faith is not an all-or-nothing thing, but that it can be achieved by degrees from the small to the large.

How can this be? It is because our connection to God is through a number of spiritual centers within our bodies that can be functioning at various levels of effectiveness. Even after we find God, we can come to a vastly greater God consciousness by developing these centers. Toward this end, most religions seek to build on our initial contact with God by providing a path to a deeper and more profound relationship with Him. This is always based on increasing the focus on the higher spiritual centers such as the heart rather than the lower centers that house our baser instincts. We can do this through time tested religious, spiritual and monastic practices that probably make no overt reference to the centers of consciousness, but nonetheless affect them, or by learning to raise the functionality of our spiritual faculties through an understanding of the architecture of the human soul, and then by acting on that understanding.

An important element of this book is to demystify our spiritual architecture so that people can better understand their own inner landscapes and how their religions work within that system to improve their interaction with God. This architecture has been described in many books, but it is usually clouded in obscure Sanskrit terminology or made fantastic by bizarre, colorful diagrams of the various centers of consciousness, or chakras. This esoteric language and imagery often do more to obscure these very natural, self-evident elements of our energetic anatomy than to reveal them. Simply put, it is easier to merely feel the emotions within the heart than to visualize some colorful swirling wheel that some book says is supposed to be there.

There is no doubt that these seven centers of consciousness *are* real, and the best and surest way to understand them is simply to feel them, note the locations of their special types of feelings, and note their obvious influences on our behaviors and choices. This is easy because feeling them, reacting to them, and hopefully balancing their often-conflicting urges is what we already do every day of our lives. We just have to be told where to examine our feelings and what to look for, and all will be clear and unarguable. Then we can use this knowledge within the envelope of our existing religion to make the most of its teachings, and also to better understand the teachings of the other faiths.

For many years our more enlightened religious leaders, as well as some secular authorities, have been pleading for tolerance between the world's great faiths. But tolerance, although a move in the right direction, is an inadequate objective because the word implies a grudging acceptance at best. One can only tolerate something for which one has some underlying measure of distaste. Tolerance, then, is often little more than a leaky dike that attempts to hold back a sea of deeply-rooted negativity, misunderstanding, feelings of superiority, and even downright hatred toward those of other faiths. It should be no surprise, that with only tolerance as the goal, efforts to promote interfaith harmony have been less than successful. We have to aim higher than that.

So, it's time for the believers in the world's major religions to go beyond mere tolerance for each other and actually come to appreciate the other faiths, and to learn from each other the gifts that God has bestowed on all of them. Believers need to learn that all of the great faiths are the spiritual bastions of their respective cultures, and in most cases, the populations of large geographical regions. All have been formative influences guiding the lives of hundreds of millions or even billions of people and all have withstood the test of time. The existence of all the major religions *is* the will of God, yes, something that He has had an active hand in, and we must come to treat them as such. The same holds for many minor religions, but as for some of the world's cults, many are more cults of personality than anything else, and one must be careful with which cult one becomes involved in, because some have become suicidal, which is only possible when an effective rite of passage has made their adherents true believers who will follow their cult leaders claims to be speaking on God's behalf.

As believers in each religion learn about each other, they can gain understanding of how the core elements of other religions *do* function to elevate people in their own journey toward God. Once they realize that each of these core elements is a gift from God, they can learn to apply those gifts within their own Faiths to help improve their own lives and relationships with their Creator. This process can make the experience of one's own traditional Faith fuller and more enriching without in any way compromising it. Further, by broadening our understanding of other Faiths beyond tolerance into acceptance and hopefully even appreciation, this experience and knowledge may even help to ensure our survival as a people and a planet.

In order to move in this direction, first we all must learn a simple truth:

God doesn't welcome you because your religion is perfect and the one way, He welcomes you even though your understanding of it falls short.

By far the most profound and life-altering experience that people can have is to come into real contact with the Divine. Generally, this happens through application of the beliefs and practices of their Faith until the Faith's rite of passage brings about feelings of worthiness. But problems can arise even from this deeply positive experience because when God becomes manifest to an individual, it is almost always attributed to the religion itself and its *specific* beliefs, scriptures, doctrines and practices. This is in a sense true, since the Faith has provided a means by which people can judge that they've become worthy to find God. But one of the primary sources of our problems on this planet is that the person then makes the incorrect assumption, that *if he or she has found God through this religion*, then it must be *the* way, and even *the only way*.

In other words, since the believer's faith "worked," the belief arises that all other, and thus different, faiths must be incorrect at best, or at worst, abominations in the eyes of God.

None of us should have vanity and false pride about the superiority of our religious beliefs and practices. Have some real faith and trust in God, that in wisdom far beyond our understanding, He has provided the world's great peoples with the truths and faiths they've needed to survive, develop and worship in ways appropriate to their times, places, cultures and historical needs.

He has not allowed billions of children to be raised under major religions that are ruinously false, or who must depend on a chance meeting with a foreign missionary to learn what is right and what's wrong. Have a modicum of faith in God that He is far, far better than that. Do not insult your Creator that He has allowed such lies in His name.

Some would answer that their religion is the only true religion because it was revealed by God, and thus its scriptures are literally true in every word. But even if our scriptures are revealed and perfect, our understanding of them cannot be perfect because as humans we all lack the wisdom of the Divine to perfectly interpret those inspired words. So, let's cast off the belief that because we have a Divinely revealed scripture, our understanding of God is somehow "better" than that of others.

Above all, please remember that other people believe just as deeply in their own faiths as you do in yours, and may even believe that yours is false. Sadly, followers of most faiths share this flaw, and while God forgives all, even this incredible hubris, God's forgiveness does not necessarily mitigate the effect that this narrow-minded view has on our world.

Time is growing short for all of us to become the harmonious family of man that God intends. If mankind is going to establish the new worldwide political and economic principles and institutions we so badly need, we must first establish a new religious and spiritual inter-faith understanding because on Earth, all things come from God and spirit. If we fail, the consequences will be unbearable for us and our progeny.

The signs are all around us. Much as ongoing financial problems can cause arguments in even the best marriages, deep and prolonged economic troubles on a worldwide scale, as we are seeing in the current millennium, can heat up the differences and conflicts between nations, cultures and faiths to beyond the boiling point.

There are those who believe that an apocalypse or Armageddon is prophesized, inevitable and impending, that the destruction of the world is part of God's plan for the near future. Some even wait for it and some actually welcome it. If we destroy our world in a nuclear holocaust, it will not be God's doing, but our own, and it will not be pleasing to our Creator. The vast majority of the people on Earth are religious, they revere God, and they pray to Him — a just God wouldn't destroy these people for the sins of others, but that doesn't mean He'll stop us from doing it, remember He's still resting.

God has imbued our spirit with a free will that is, along with our spirit, the crown of creation. Just as we've used our free will to induce an accelerating movement toward the destruction of all mankind, we can now apply our free will to reverse it. To do so, we must immediately begin to move toward appreciation for those great, even noble, qualities that enable each of the world's major religions to bring people into a genuine relationship with God.

If enough believers can come to understand the validity and value of other faiths, then we can start to multiply those numbers toward critical mass by using global communication tools such as the various forms of social media. Right now, the herd instinct works against interfaith understanding, but if people recognize that a more positive consensus is forming, many more will jump on board.

The goal is for more people to learn how to think and act not just as individuals, not just as members of groups such as nationalities, or as members of a religion, *but as one, as members of the tribe of humanity*. For the human race ever to truly become "mankind," which implies the existence of one all encompassing group, we must put all our differences in proper perspective, including, and especially, the differences in our religions. Nothing could be farther from God's will than for mankind to remain divided over how to worship Him.

Warfare between religions is as old as history, and now with nuclear weapons available to some of the currently likely combatants, the level of danger to all humanity is unprecedented. Conflicts over ideology, economics and empire that loomed over the latter twentieth century, our current century and the centuries before sometimes lent themselves more readily to pragmatic solutions, because unlike trying to reconcile disagreements between faiths, political or economic compromise did not seem a betrayal of one's obligations to God. But the truth is that it is not betraying God to put the preservation of His creation and His creatures ahead of stubborn allegiance to ancient and misunderstood codifications of our belief systems.

And although this book advocates appreciating other faiths, we do not suggest here that anyone abandon even the slightest detail of their own traditional religious observances. Appreciating other faiths does not mean lessening our full commitment to our own beliefs, whether deeply or casually held, and which are true in their ability to bring us to God where we can derive so much comfort and joy.

The roots of our traditional faiths are embedded deeply in our psyches because, in many cases, these beliefs were taught to us by family, church and culture perhaps since infancy. People who move away from their family's faith during adolescence or young adulthood often find great comfort in returning to it later, as if they are coming home again. So do not "leave home," that is, do not leave the Faith of your parents and ancestors. It has brought you to God, and if it has not done so yet, it can.

An example of this is the millions of young people who turned to hedonism under the influence of the counter culture in the sixties or seventies, or perhaps moved away from Christianity to gravitate toward secular humanism under the influence of academic and cultural modernism. Probably in college, they became convinced that their religion was just a *mélange* of silly superstitions, that the accounts in its scriptures were myths and fables, and that its Savior or Prophet was little more than a failed and frustrated social revolutionary.

In time, however, many of these people found that they'd moved into a cold, empty space. They felt insecurity, isolation and deep loneliness in their hearts. At some point, they came face-to-face with an uncomforted fear of death and what comes after. They felt the big chill of their own fragility, mortality and separateness. When exposed to charismatic, born-again Christianity, millions embraced this exciting, fresher version of their family's faith and the hope it offered with a fervency that has transformed American culture and continues to provide believers with a deep, comforting sense of God's love decades later.

The wisest choice for anyone is to seek truth and meaning within the framework of their own traditional faith. Consequently, it also must be said that while one of the thrusts of this book is to harmonize religion, it absolutely does not want to do so by attempting to found a new one. There are plenty enough religions already.

It is also important for people of all faiths to realize that their scriptures were revealed to their ancestors in the context of very different times and places. All should examine their traditional interpretations of their scriptures and try to view them in the context of the world we now live in, the scientific knowledge that God has revealed to us, and the dangers that this same science has created through the technologies it fostered. By so doing, we can deepen our commitment to our own Faith by broadening our understanding of its place in the tapestry of God's vast web of revelations to all mankind.

13: WHAT'S BEHIND THE WORLD'S SIX GREAT FAITHS

There are perhaps hundreds of faiths on our planet, many of them with many millions of adherents, now or in their histories, such as Taoism, Shinto, Sikhism and Confucianism. However, there are six belief systems, five of them traditional religions and one a much more modern belief system, which have had, and continue to have, the greatest influence on today's world. These six also, to a great extent, define cultures, peoples, nations and eras. They also encompass most of the effective practices and modalities that may be utilized across religious boundaries, as we grow to understand the workings of the six major faiths we'll describe.

Each of the great traditional religions was gifted by God to certain peoples because of their unique needs in very specific times and places. Now these religions' followers must come to realize that those specific times and places have changed as has our ability to understand our place in the universe.

For all religions, the task now at hand is to free God's revelations from the strictures and limits imposed by the ancient times, original locations and primitive mindsets of their beginnings. But to do this while not losing the essential, functional and effective core of their beliefs and practices. In short, all Faiths must now learn to adapt their teachings to today's world, and this creates the opportunity to share knowledge with, and learn from, each other.

The world's great traditional religions are Christianity, Islam, Hinduism, Judaism and Buddhism. All are perfect in their ability to use their own unique rite of passage to bring a person into contact with the Supreme Being, whether called God, Allah, Yahweh, Brahma, or in the case of Buddhism, the Absolute.

These five major faiths have been joined, over the past few decades, by a new belief system, a system that rose up and at first seemed to challenge, rather than fortify, the great faiths' answers to some of man's most profound questions. This system is Science, and as its discoveries unfold, once again, God is providing a font of knowledge, wisdom and truth, and we should not ignore His new revelations, some of which bear on the big questions such as: How did the universe begin? How did the planet Earth come to be? How did we humans come to be?

Answering these questions has always been irrelevant to helping a person to find God — this process depends on the religion's rite of passage. Yet for largely good reasons, most religions have attempted to provide these answers anyway. But sadly, the answers they've provided have become calcified, unchanging and unresponsive to newer information that God continually reveals to us on an almost daily basis. Worse, these ancient, calcified answers have become so identified in people's minds with the religions that offer them that many people do not believe a relationship with God is possible unless they believe in these stories. But the truth is that God will not accept or reject you based on your belief in any particular version of cosmic history. You can connect to God more readily as a truth seeker than as a blind believer.

Over the past few hundreds of years, Science, as an institution, has by turns been agnostic, atheistic and even profane. But now it has at last become a channel for God's continuing revelations in a way that can fortify, rather than attack, the traditional faiths. So, while Science is not usually regarded as a religion, it offers answers to many of the same questions as do religions and as a primary belief system, it has hundreds of millions if not billions of adherents. It has also recently developed a nascent but growing ability to bring some of the world's most intelligent and previously skeptical people literally face-to-face with God. There has come to be an incredible sense of wonder that some scientists are feeling as their expanding knowledge brings them closer to some incredible cosmic truths that are beginning to reveal God to them. This is giving science its own viable rite of passage to feelings of religious worthiness for many of them. They know that they have a profound knowledge of the nature of the universe, and once they realize that they've found God in their science, they can find Him in their hearts.

Unfortunately, the gap between the atheistic belief system that science has previously been and the nascent scientific religion that it's becoming is huge. But fortunately, that gap is closing, as typified by scientists' name for an elusive sub-atomic particle that they have finally generated in their giant particle accelerators, the elusive Higgs Boson, which many scientists have called The God Particle.

The Variety of Rites of Passage

At their cores, all faiths work in their own unique ways to affect the believer's receptivity to God, and not God's receptivity to the believer, which is constant. We are not going to change God, but what we can change is ourselves. To reiterate how this happens, each faith functions through its own unique "rite of passage" which, if performed successfully and sincerely, makes seekers feel that they have become worthy of a relationship with God. This rite of passage can be, depending on the religion, finding *faith* for Christians, *submitting* to Allah for Muslims, maintaining *righteousness* for Jews, achieving *acceptance* and finally *transcendence* for Buddhists, or gaining spiritual *knowledge* by activating the centers of consciousness for Hindus. As seekers come to feel worthy because they've performed their rites of passage, they set aside the guilt, shame and self-loathing, or whatever other negative feelings have separated them from what has always been inside: God's presence.

In other words, through adherence to the path of their traditional religion, they come to perform its rite of passage to their own satisfaction, and then they can feel that they've become worthy of having a relationship with God. Once they've gained that feeling of worthiness, there is no more impediment to facing God, and they can simply let themselves become aware of His overwhelmingly obvious presence. Thus, through whatever their religion, and whatever its rite of passage, they can genuinely find God and the resulting experience can be completely transformative.

Of course, for all the best of reasons, they want to share their successful experience, their effective path to God, with others. Over the centuries this positive desire to share their religions' successful path has manifested in benign forms such as missionary work and proselytizing and less benign forms from inquisition to *jihad*. Knowing that their religions' paths reached the goal of coming to God, these people, whose experiences have made them true believers, assume that all other paths are false. And this single tragic assumption is the cause of much of the world's pain and is what drives our drift toward the precipice of destruction. Think of the Christian catch phrase "One Way," which we'll discuss below, to understand how exclusionary their beliefs often become due to the profound success of their own religious practices. Thus, they have no reason to explore, let alone come to understand, other faiths.

Following are short summaries of the major religions, their rites of passage, and how they enable people to find God.

Christianity

The faithful of Christianity number over two billion people to make it the numerically largest religion in the world. It is also dominant within some of the world's most powerful and advanced cultures and nations. Precisely because of its cultural dominance, it is vital that Christians find a way to understand and embrace the other faiths. Sadly, this is especially difficult for Christians as it is a tenet of

Christian doctrine, adhered to by many, that their way is the "one way" and that all other religions are false. This is an interesting issue because there is a solid, if subtle, element of truth in their belief. What can be called Christ Consciousness is actually the sixth chakra and accessing it does not really require the instrumentality of, or belief in, Jesus. This aspect of our spiritual anatomy is the only way to fully access the seventh chakra which is God's tendril into us. Remember Jesus saying in Matthew 6:22, "...if therefore thine eye be single, thy whole body shall be full of light..." Christians can reach the sixth chakra and their name for this singular road to God is "the Son of God" which to them is also a personification named Jesus or Yeshua.

The problem is that while their beliefs enable an efficient access to the sixth chakra and then God, their insistence that the still extant personage of Jesus, *is the only way to God.* Christianity does "understand" how this connection works and does a remarkably good job of enabling its adherents to successfully navigate this inner journey, their particular mythology, language and imagery for this process notwithstanding. It is most important to know that it is Christian doctrine, codified at the Council of Nicaea, that the aspect of God called Christ has always existed and thus could not have come into existence through the personage of Jesus. Of course, most Christians don't actually realize this crucial element of their doctrinal belief system and consider Christ to be something that came into existence upon the birth of Jesus. So, if a Christian follows the actual dictates of their own faith, they would know that Christ, let's jump to the phrase "Christ Consciousness", predated Jesus by however many years one believes the universe to have existed. The belief that Christ was a creation of God was called Arianism and was officially made a heresy at the above-referenced Council of Nicaea. But most Christians don't realize all this, that it is actually a formal article of Christian belief, and correctly so, that Christ has existed as part of God even before the creation, so it follows that Christ must predate its embodiment as Jesus. But Christians almost all just go to incorrectly equating the spirit and idea of Christ with the life and personage of Jesus. But deeper in Christianity is the knowledge that the spirit of Christ is something universal that predates Jesus and has always been a part of God. Yes, this is the sixth chakra, the one way to God, but no, you do not need to be a Christian to find that path.

Thus, although they did not use the word Christ, holy men such as Moses could not have reached God if they hadn't first realized the sixth chakra, what might today be called "Christ Consciousness," the only path to the Divine, through their own inner journeys. Likewise, other religions can bring people into this spiritual presence or level which pre-dates and transcends the personage of Jesus.

Christianity brings people close to God through faith, a powerful and effective rite of passage, although not an easy one. This is because faith is an active process that must be jumpstarted by the religious novice, and even when established, must build and feed on itself as it takes root and grows. And to make the process even more difficult, this faith is not just in something invisible, but in something that will not become manifest until that faith is complete! This, at first, can be difficult to muster, let alone master, sometimes requiring a great deal of prayer, devotion and meditation before it can bring the reward of a transformative religious experience.

To help this very difficult process to work, God put Jesus on the Earth. As was discussed previously, the non-locality of the holographic universe proves that there is a very real connection between all humans that spans space and time to eliminate all divisions between people, and Jesus is no exception. The connection to Jesus that Christians feel, then is not imaginary or supernatural, but is grounded in these recent and undeniable scientific discoveries. Once connected to Jesus, we can all benefit from His special channel to God that is the great gift of Christianity. This is what makes the very difficult Christian rite of passage of faith achievable, but sadly, it is also what makes them believe that without Jesus, and faith in Him, no connection to God can be made.

When faith finally reaches critical mass, it lights a fire in the human heart, creating what Christians call the state of grace. With the help of Christian teachings that faith and grace can offer forgiveness of all sins, the resulting sense of purity is so strong that it can sweep away all impediments to someone's relationship with God. In short, they feel more than worthy enough to turn to God, and of course God is there, where is God not?

Thus, the world's billions of Christians are truly brought into contact with God, and it doesn't matter if they're Protestants, Catholics, Seventh Day Adventists or Baptists, the underlying means of achieving this contact with God is the same, fulfilling the rite of passage of faith through the holographically available spirit of Jesus.

Christianity's rise to its position as the world's largest religion proves the efficacy of faith as a reliable and true rite of passage. The fervency and certainty of its believers first became apparent with

Christianity's early martyrs, who faced agonizing death with a calmness that transfixed their Roman onlookers. This fervency continues today among missionaries who face danger and even death to work for the salvation of others.

Christianity also imbues a moral sense that is best stated as "love thy neighbor as thyself." This moral sense is based on Jewish law, but since the days of the Apostle Paul, Christians have used that law only as a guidepost, and have been guided in their moral choices by the grace that comes with their faith.

But within Christianity there remains a strand of direct adherence to God's laws, and this can be found in the New Testament's Book of James. Thus, we can understand the Apostle Paul not to be advocating abandonment of all Jewish laws, but rather release from some of the stricter laws that include things such as dietary restrictions. Common sense guides most Christians in this direction, and thus, most of them will have no problem with eating pork, but still believe in following the Ten Commandments. However, they do not believe that their salvation, or connection to God, comes from positive actions, or "good works," but rather from their faith itself.

Christianity started as a pure belief system, but after its establishment as the official religion of the Roman Empire, it took on a decidedly political aspect. At the Council of Nicaea, Christianity made a sharp move away from being a pluralistic community of diverse beliefs to becoming a monolithic and somewhat authoritarian institution under the direction of an infallible leader – the Pope. Later, it became such a worldly political institution that it even came to raise and field armies of conquest during the Crusades. Throughout the

Inquisition, the witch trials, and at other times, the Christians frequently persecuted and tortured those who held divergent beliefs, much as they had been persecuted themselves. It even waged war against fellow Christians, such as the Cathars of southern France, who believed in "heresies" and were annihilated for it. So, when Christians criticize the warlike histories of other faiths, in particular Islam, they should also look to the violent history of their own faith, and realize that it is the human element within the faith, not the faith itself, that causes any violent tendencies.

Later, starting with the Protestant reformation, Christianity again became increasingly pluralistic with an ever-growing number of divisions, and this brought centuries of internal or civil warfare between people who all claimed belief in Christ and God. But through this entire process, believers in all the strands of Christianity continued to personally find God. This is because the Christian rite of passage continued in its efficacy, with the help of quantum entanglement with Jesus, no matter what doctrinal shifts or realignments occurred.

Islam

Islam means submission, and it is the world's fastest growing religion because submission to God is a passive act of surrender, and thus a very easy and natural rite of passage. It can reach full force almost instantly without having to build on itself as does faith. That's why Mohammed does not have to intercede, as does Jesus, as a personal spiritual force to help people achieve their religions' rites of passage. Thus, he can be viewed as a prophet and teacher rather than as a spiritual bridge or aspect of God. Mohammed's discovery of submission as what we are calling a "rite of passage" ranks as one of the most brilliant breakthroughs in the history of mankind. Submission is such an easy and effective rite of passage that it's almost like throwing a switch, and then one feels as if they've fallen into the hands of God.

The extreme efficacy of submission as a religious system marks Islam as a great and true faith that has brought over a billion people into a genuine relationship with God. Christians, please at least look at the fervency of these fellow God believers, even unto intentional death. They are not pretending.

As the world's second largest religion, it is dominant over major geographic regions encompassing many cultures, including some that have, at times, been among the most powerful in the world such as Persia, Turkey (Ottoman Empire) and Egypt. Today, Islam is the primary faith within well over fifty nations, many of them very powerful, wealthy and influential. But like Christianity, Islam sadly tends to instill a belief that those who follow other faiths are in error, and correcting this error, even by force, can be for their own good.

This provides a very dangerous rationale for coercive and even forceful conversions to Islam. In fact, Islam's initial spread was through the use of force after the prophet Mohammed raised a large army and forced non-believers to convert at the point of the sword. Of course, as a believer himself, Mohammed "knew" that he was doing these converts a vital favor. This forceful approach to spreading the faith continued for centuries and almost resulted in the conquest and conversion of Europe.

But in spite of this history, and in spite of the fact that Islamic forces are involved in many, if not most, of the world's current armed conflicts, much "Islamic" violence today is not actually related to attempts to spread the faith through force. Most is more related to attempts to gain self-determination for areas that are already Islamic, or once were, such as Israel/Palestine. Islam thus is not just a religion, but also a political or governmental system, including the establishment of the Islamic *sharia* law. In the Middle East, the violence is concerned primarily with issues arising from the establishment and defense of the current state of Israel and the stationing of troops in Muslim nations by Western non-Muslim powers. Since these are political problems that do have religious roots and overtones, they present the danger of spawning highly-charged religiously oriented solutions, such as *jihad.*

Another primary driving force behind Islam's more general, non-regionalized conflicts with the Judeo-Christian world is a sense of frustration in the face of the perceived cultural, political and military subordination of the Islamic world to the Judeo-Christian civilization. This is not to say that were the tables turned and Islam were to become dominant culturally, politically and especially militarily, that the impulse to assert that dominance to empower forceful religious conversion would not recur. But that situation is extremely unlikely if not impossible in the foreseeable future, so "Islamic" violence remains a political weapon that attempts to use religion as a rallying cry, rather than the real geopolitical reason driving Palestinian aspirations, for example – even this not being a primarily religious phenomenon.

Sadly, there is also a great deal of violence between followers of the two primary divisions within Islam, the Sunnis and the Shiites. For both groups, the core beliefs are the same, the rite of passage through submission is identical, and there is no argument that both worship the same God they call Allah, although over the years their religious practices have diverged somewhat.

The schism between them dates back to a leadership struggle that followed the death of the Prophet Mohammed. The word Sunni comes from an Arabic word that means "one who follows the traditions of the prophet." Upon Mohammed's death, many of his close companions believed that the next leader of the faith should be elected from candidates they deemed worthy of that leadership position. One of Mohammed's closest friends and most trusted advisors, Abu Bakr was elected to be the Caliph of the Islamic nation.

But the group who would become Shia Muslims believed that leadership should remain in Mohammed's family, and put their weight behind the leadership of his cousin and son-in-law, Ali. The word "Shia" is a shortened form of *Shia-t-Ali*, or the Party of Ali. The Shiites did not accept the authority of the elected Sunni leaders, since they were clearly elected by men. Instead, they followed Imams whom they believed were appointed by God Himself, albeit through Mohammed or other human instrumentalities.

Following from this initial difference, the current beliefs of the two groups differ somewhat, especially in regard to the degree of veneration afforded their leaders. Since Shiites view their Imams as deriving authority directly from God, they consider them to be sinless and infallible much as Catholics view the Pope. After their deaths, they are venerated as Saints who can help Shia Muslims to get their prayers answered.

The Sunnis today continue to disparage the idea of hereditary privilege within Islam, and believe that leadership must be earned, with judgment coming from the authority of the people. There is no veneration of, or prayer to, sainted former leaders.

In addition to the Quran, Sunni Islam is based on texts called Hadith that were eye witness accounts of what Mohammed did and what he said. It must be remarked that since the authors of the Hadith were among the close companions of Mohammed who began the Sunni traditions, the Hadith are not regarded as holy texts by Shiites.

This schism in Islam provides a textbook example of how the politics and doctrinal differences within a religion or between religions are completely irrelevant to its efficacy. The rite of passage, submission, remains the same for both Shiite and Sunni, and its practice enables followers of both branches of Islam to feel equally worthy of opening to God. Who can think that God would discriminate between equally devout Muslims based on the historical and geographical accidents of their belief in one process of succession or the other? Does it matter which is correct? In fact, is either one the only way which is correct and the other false? Does it really matter at all? Of course not, all that matters is that a Muslim sincerely believes in his faith and comes to feel worthy of God by performing his faith's beautifully and uniquely effective rite of passage.

Judaism

As most of us know, Judaism is the well-spring of Christianity and Islam, and as such is the source of their monotheism. It is also the source of all three faiths' unique understandings of God's laws. It's rite of passage is righteousness through adherence to Jewish law.

Depending on the type of Judaism in question, this rite of passage can be difficult and hard to maintain, or extremely difficult and tediously demanding, but in no case is it easy, nor in any case is it impossible. But according the stories that are related in its scriptures, it has never been easy.

The Jewish concept of righteousness is the mother of all Western rites of passage, and it provides clear guidelines by which a person can judge the degree of their own success. But in spite of its rigorous demands, most Jews find that they can meet the demands of their faith for righteousness and can thus feel worthy of finding God within. However, many Jews are non-observant, so they do not seek the benefits of this rite of passage.

Although the Jews were clearly chosen by God to bring monotheism and the treasures of His laws, in particular the Ten Commandments, to the world, ironically they were able to do so, for many billions of people, primarily through the spread of religions that only derived from Judaism. These religions, to wit Christianity and Islam, did at least contain much of its messages such as the Ten Commandments, So, while Jewish monotheism and holy laws such as the Ten Commandments have now reached, informed and edified much of the world, the Jewish religion itself was constrained in its growth by ties to specific national, cultural and even genetic limitations. This is why most people who have learned of God's commandments have done so in a Christian church or a Muslim mosque, not a Jewish synagogue.

Righteousness, the rite of passage of Judaism, requires rigorous learning and study to first come to understand God's laws, and secondly it requires strictly following them by performing good works. It also requires rituals of penance to address their deficiencies. But by following the path of Judaism, a person can come to feel that they have become worthy of walking with God, and once feeling worthy, they can establish a relationship. This is the rite of passage of Judaism.

It should not go unremarked that by devoting themselves to following God's laws and living an upright and righteous life, they often pass their time on Earth as exemplary human beings. This is one of their many gifts to humanity.

All of us owe a tremendous spiritual debt to the Jews, as well as our respect, because they have maintained their faith and beliefs in the face of millennia of unimaginable hardships. The pain they've faced in spite of their special place in our world has forced them to look deeply into man's relationship with God and further expand their knowledge and wisdom.

They withstood wholesale assaults on their homeland by pagans, Moslems and Christians, including their wholesale banishment from the Holy Land by the Roman Empire for around 20 centuries. They withstood the Inquisition in Europe that attempted to decimate them as a people and a faith, followed by numerous pogroms and ultimately the Holocaust. Now they resist creeping anti-Semitism as it manifests in various nations from Japan to France including the United States, not to mention the Islamic nations.

The wisdom that God has bequeathed to them, and that they have in turn bequeathed to the world, was forged in the crucible of the endless persecution, torture and genocide against them, both modern and ancient. This wisdom is a precious gift to us all. Without the Jews, we might all still be worshipping stone idols and golden calves. We might never have learned the profound laws revealed by God that seem like simple common sense to some of us now, but that were groundbreaking innovations in the days of Moses.

We can continue to learn from Judaism in other ways. Cabalistic Judaism long ago developed a vision of the relationship between man and God that parallels the vision that is presented in this book. This relationship is now being verified by science as it digs so deeply into nature, whether with microscopes, telescopes or particle accelerators, that it must of course eventually find at its core, at its alpha and omega, the infinite Creator, the one God first of the Jews and now of us all.

Hinduism

The rite of passage of Hinduism is to perform physical, mental and spiritual exercises that directly activate the spiritual centers which enable and enhance our connection to God. Although in some ways this is the most direct and simple of all the rites of passage, it is certainly not the easiest. It can require years of hard work to bear its full fruit, but when the connection to God is established, it will be a high bandwidth holy hookup that Jesus would never refer to as "of little faith."

Although not generally considered a monotheistic religion, much like most denominations of Christianity, Hinduism teaches that there is a great Trinity. Brahma is the creator aspect of this Trinity who brought the universe and all life into being. Vishnu is the preserver that protects the world and its cycle of life. Shiva is the destroyer.

Before rejecting this as being so different from western monotheism, one must ask if these attributes of God are not part and parcel of our monotheistic traditions, while clearly paralleling Christian Trinitarian orthodoxy. Whoever has read the Judeo-Christian Bible can recognize all these aspects of God in its pages. Even God's face as a destroyer is manifest from time to time throughout biblical history. As the destroyer, He culled humanity with the great flood and, according to the Old Testament, brought a rain of fire down on Sodom and Gomorrah. And of course, He made the walls of Jericho come tumbling down. As the sustainer, He brought manna to the Jews during the exodus. As the creator, He brought the universe, the planet and mankind into existence in Genesis.

Hinduism also personifies and deifies many other aspects of God's relationship to man and the world, some nurturing, some corrective, and this plethora of names and images further obscures Hinduism's kinship to the monotheistic faiths. However, we can understand that the powers represented by many of these deities are no more than names for *aspects* of a monotheistic God.

Unlike most other religions, Hinduism cannot trace its origins to a singular prophet/founder or a singular primary scripture. In fact, along with its Trinity of principal Gods, Hinduism also has a Trinity of sacred scriptures: the *Vedas*, the *Upanishads* and the *Bhagavad Gita*, literally "The Song of God," a name which in its use of the singular proper noun hints at some of the monotheistic currents within.

However, Hinduism's value to others lies, not so much in the nuances of its theology, but in the efficacy of its practices. Its status as the most ancient of all of today's faiths has left it the guardian of some of God's most enlightening and fundamental truths, especially about the inner workings and architecture of the human spirit or psyche.

Hinduism has within it, Yoga, and this is a body of knowledge and practices that might best be described as religious or spiritual technologies. Drawing on great knowledge of the structure of spirit, it seeks to transform and refine lower, baser human qualities into those that are higher, nobler and ultimately sacred. But in spite of its Hindu origins, Yoga can be, and is being, practiced in the context of "other" religions including Christianity.

Hinduism at its best works through this very special, esoteric knowledge, related to amplifying and energizing the spiritual structures within us that enable our spiritual advancement and connection to God. Hindu esoteric knowledge is concerned with increasing the energy in our higher centers, including those responsible for the strength or size of our faith and God consciousness. What would Christians think if they knew that Hinduism's religious technology could help them to address the two thousand years old complaint of their Savior about the magnitude of their faith?

Hinduism can do this by helping us understand how our very souls actually function, how they are affected by positive practices such as worship and negative practices such as dissipation. This knowledge can be used to shift our attentions and energies from our lower to our higher spiritual centers. There is a Hindu word for these spiritual centers that we have used extensively here because it has been brought into the English language and has entered our culture from Masonic doctrine to children's anime cartoons: "chakras." By bringing this formerly esoteric knowledge into world culture, Hinduism can help us to understand how our own religions actually work, and how to make them work better.

Buddhism

The rite of passage of Buddhism is a process of acceptance of all things, and this acceptance ultimately leads to transcendence from worldly concerns and connection with what Buddhists call the Absolute. Like the Hindu path, this is rigorous, and requires a great deal of meditation and inner work. But it is a viable rite of passage that can bring adherents into the presence of what to Buddhists is the Supreme Being, although they don't seem to personify the Absolute the way other faiths seem to personify God.

Mahayana is the dominant strain of Buddhism in northern India, China, Japan, Korea and other areas of Asia. It is also more prevalent among adherents to Buddhism in the West. It has primarily superseded the more monastic and severe *Theravada* form which remains dominant only in southern India and Sri Lanka.

Buddhists don't consider the Absolute to be a personal, willful and actively involved God, but instead a constant, unchanging quality of the universe that while at the root of all consciousness, does not intervene or judge. This means that our actions and thoughts are left to create their own outcomes.

This is karma, the law of cause and effect, another word from Eastern religion that has become part of the common English language. But thinking about cause and effect, we can quickly realize that not all effects or outcomes are desirable. That means that some causes, or actions have effects that are not in our best interests. So, while the Buddhist Absolute does not judge, nonetheless in place are mechanisms that in effect do the judging automatically. The effect is clearly the same, or to put karma into Christian terms, karma can be "the wages of sin." Or the rewards of virtue.

The modality of Buddhism is acceptance of all aspects of life, resulting in transcendence of our worldly bonds. Through this transcendence we can reach enlightenment or Nirvana, a state of complete identification with the Universal or Absolute, a concept perhaps easily understood by Westerners as similar to the Native American concept of "The Great Spirit."

In defense of the Buddhist conception of the Absolute, it could be argued that personifying a willful, interventionist God, as do the conventionally monotheistic Western faiths, is to anthropomorphize a Being that is actually far beyond human understanding. Following this thinking then, attributing personality, will, judgment and other human qualities to God may be farther from explaining the unexplainable than is the Buddhist view, wherein the Absolute remains ineffable and beyond our comprehension. Perhaps accepting this fundamental mystery as to God's nature can help us all to accept the contradictions within our own understanding of the Divine.

For example, one of the great challenges that all religions face is to explain injustice and human suffering in the context of our conception of a loving, all-knowing and all-powerful God. For example, why does God let a school bus carrying dozens of innocent Christian school children drive off a road and down a cliff, killing or maiming many of them?

Yet such disasters do strike the innocent, not to mention world wars, great plagues and deadly natural catastrophes, and it's hard to imagine that these broad strokes of suffering and death are so selective in their targeting as to strike only the guilty and the deserving of punishment, whatever that means. Without doubt, the innocent do suffer as all must someday die, no matter their virtues.

Does Buddhism offer helpful answers to the challenge of coping with these harsh realities? Can their answers be integrated into other faiths? The answer is yes, because Buddhism emphasizes acceptance of suffering as an inevitable reality of life and does not blame the Absolute for these things, but rather a combination of the nature of life itself, man's free will and the mysteries of karma.

But lacking a personal God to whom to turn, how does Buddhist acceptance bring comfort, joy and love? In contrast, Western faiths provide a God that is a father-figure, and our relationship with Him a virtual mimicking of our childlike faith in the warmth and protection of loving parents. This is an obvious and explicit statement in our religious terminology, as in "Heavenly Father." Perhaps Buddhists could find comfort in seeking a connection to these more personal and emotionally comforting aspects of the Absolute which are there for the benefit of all, as other religions might demonstrate.

If our need for a Divine stand-in parental figure is infantile, equally infantile is our slavery to desire. As adults, we don't often externalize our frustrations when our desires are thwarted as we did in our childhood temper tantrums. So, while we've learned not to display them publicly, we still have those feelings of frustration and we still formulate much of our lives in their service. It is this continuing investment in our desires, as the Buddhists know, that causes much of our worldly pain and suffering.

Buddhism teaches that through acceptance of what we have, which leads to transcendence of desire for the things we don't have, we can eliminate desire's evil twin, frustration. Through this process, we can achieve an eventual end to much of our suffering. We can try to displace emphasis on our personal desires with a focus on more positive qualities such as politeness, humanity, modesty, sensitivity to the feelings of others and generally all the basic virtues.

So even without personifying God, Buddhism recognizes that there are attitudes and actions with positive and negative results, implicitly recognizing the immutable nature of what monotheists would call God's laws. Thus, by seeing the Absolute as a singular unity that is inseparable from universal laws, Buddhism is only a semantic leap away from being a great monotheistic religion.

To summarize, Buddhism brings people to the Absolute through the process of acceptance of reality and ultimately transcendence of desire. By accepting the things they encounter and the events that they experience, they stop resisting forces greater than themselves and thus come into harmony with their own lives, the lives of others, and by extension, with the Absolute. Everyone can learn from this process.

Science

All of the great belief systems, except Science, are easily recognized as faiths, but Science has now come to the point of discovering God in the grand, cosmic patterns of the universe, the incredible and intricate genetic structures that underlie life, and the profound, almost unbelievable, quantum characteristics we, the observers, see in subatomic particles.

Thus, many scientists have found God through their various disciplines. There is a body of literature developing that makes manifest this new current in scientific thinking. Perhaps Paul Davies says it best in his book *The Mind of God: The Scientific Basis for a Rational World* when he states:

> I belong to the group of scientists who do not subscribe to a conventional religion but nevertheless deny that the universe is a purposeless accident. Through my scientific work I have come to believe more and more strongly that the physical universe is put together with an ingenuity so astonishing that I cannot accept it merely as a brute fact. There must, it seems to me, be a deeper level of explanation. Whether one wishes to call that deeper level 'God' is a matter of taste and definition. Furthermore, I have come to the point of view that mind — i.e., conscious awareness of the world — is not a meaningless and incidental quirk of nature, but an absolutely fundamental facet of reality.[5]

But even absent this recent "discovery" of God, Science is a belief system that answers many of the questions that man has asked of their faiths. How was the universe created? What is the history of Earth? What sustains us as living creatures? How did the wide range of living things come to be? This is because the modality of science as a belief system is the rigorous search for truth. A scientist feels worthiness because, within Science, truth is the greatest good, and thus seeking it makes one worthy. By seeking and finding answers to the biggest questions, Science becomes an important part of the process by which God reveals new truths to man.

If a scientist considers himself to be a genuine agent of truth and discovery, that is Science's rite of passage and its badge of worthiness, but that alone is not enough. The scientist must still choose to look inside for the door to the Divine. This requires some sort of religious inclination, since someone can't easily look for something that they don't believe exists. But scientists who can see the religious implications of their, and their colleagues', work can certainly come to feel worthy of connecting to the Divine because they know that they are agents of the truth. Because of this, they can have true religious experiences without any reference to any specific faith's doctrines, but rather from the awe they see in their own discoveries, the discoveries of others, and from the incredible universe that they perceive with unmatched clarity. And make no mistake, scientists as agents of truth are now serving God's purposes by redefining and refining our understanding of the universe, and our place in it, with new answers to some of our oldest questions.

But if recent scientific discoveries are true, and thus might be construed as revelations even though they were not written on a clay tablet, why were these answers not revealed previously by God within the great scriptures? The answer is actually quite simple. Had God revealed these truths to man previously there would have been no context within which man could have understood them. For example, Moses had no framework to understand DNA or a black hole in space. Thus, by advancing God's on-going process of revelation, Science works toward creating an ever-expanding context for greater understanding of religious truths.

It is ironic that in the field of quantum physics, Science, once the most atheistic of man's belief systems, has moved very close to literal proof of God's existence, or at least of spirit's important place in the universe. Science has learned that the quantum state of any subatomic particle is dependent on an observer. That is to say consciousness interacts directly with events in the realm of physics, indicating that consciousness is as intrinsic to the universe as are matter and energy, and that it is developing a place in our understanding of physics as well as the life sciences.

But what does the establishment of consciousness as an element of physics have to do with proving God's existence? Everything, because God is consciousness and consciousness is God. And while the existence of our own consciousness is perhaps the one thing of which we can be absolutely certain, everything else being fallible data from our senses, Science has for many years viewed it as an accident of evolution, a characteristic of certain organisms that has increased their survival value and has thus been favored and refined by natural selection over countless generations.

Nothing could be further from the truth. Life is not an accident and especially neither is consciousness. Fortunately, Science is moving toward that understanding, not just because of the revelations of quantum physics about the smallest structures of the universe, but also because of discoveries on its very largest scale, the enormous cosmic scale of astrophysics.

These discoveries in astrophysics that are moving Science toward God realization began with a very serious, and for them paradigm shattering, anomaly that astronomers discovered while observing the motions of the billions of galaxies and their relationships to each other.

They had previously surmised that all matter was set in motion by the Big Bang and that the incredible momentum generated in that primal blast has continued to drive all galaxies away from each other in the expanding universe. This expansion, from one end of the universe to the other, and at all points in between, has been experimentally verified. However, progressively more accurate measurements of the galaxies' motion revealed what seemed to some theorists to be a serious anomaly.

The unimaginably gigantic gravitational force of all the galaxies, that is, of all the matter in the universe, plus the much greater gravity of the dark matter, should inexorably pull against the momentum imparted by the Big Bang and gradually slow down the expansion. In fact, the galaxies should not only slow down, but eventually stop and even reverse their direction, finally falling towards each other's gravitational fields to create in the far distant future "The Big Crunch."

But scientists discovered that the expansion of the universe was not slowing down, and even more anomalous, the speed of every galaxy's expansion away from all others was actually increasing. Something more powerful than the combined gravitational force of all the galaxies in the universe plus the dark matter was continuing to drive them away from each other, even accelerating their expansion.

This effect would have to derive from some force of unimaginable power, literally the strongest force in all the universe.

Because this force is invisible, most scientists began to call it "Dark Energy." However, other scientists have labeled this force as "Quintessence," perhaps a more appealing name for an all-powerful force which opposes the entropic power of gravity and thus drives the expansion and preservation of the universe. Now the question must arise: Was it this force that powered that expansion from the very beginning of creation and fueled the Big Bang itself? If so, can this force be identified as an observable manifestation of the Creator?

Another aspect of Science that has religious implications is the discovery of DNA. Now that we know that life is based on a molecule with the shape of a double helix, we can compare the centrality of this unusual shape to the double helix that is a symbol of our medical profession, as well as other "coiled serpent" mythologies and imagery from various traditions worldwide, such as the Hindu Kundalini. Scientists, with their knowledge of resonance, may well see a relationship between the double helixes of spiritual tradition and the double helix they've discovered that forms the center of every cell of our bodies.

It's not hard to see why so many scientists are now thinking about God!

14: HOW TO PREVENT FUTURE WARS

To many people our world seems to be on the verge of entering into what some call the "End Days." Some people believe that the approaching end of the world will come at God's direction through the Judeo-Christian concept of Armageddon, and while some fear these events, others actually look forward to them and can't wait for the coming "rapture," with millions believing they will be some of the 144,000 who will bodily rise to heaven.

Others dread the possibility of an extermination event caused by the impact of an asteroid or comet such as evidently resulted in the extinction of the dinosaurs. Some subscribe to the Internet rumor that our planet will soon be spinning off its axis because of a close fly-by of the unknown planet Nibiru. Nibiru is supposedly on a highly elliptical orbit that keeps it far out in space until it flies deep into the solar system at the apex of its huge ellipse, its gravity disrupting the other planets along the way. Many people laugh at, but others fear, an unspecified, but still deadly, event that is famously predicted by the Mayan calendar.

Many others fear that secret cabals are planning massive depopulation via a man-made pandemic. Less conspiratorial people fear extermination by a natural pandemic. Many are aware of the inevitable eruption of the super-volcano caldera under the Yellowstone National Park, and think that if it follows its historic pattern, it will destroy North America relatively soon. It will also impact the rest of the world with a non-nuclear "nuclear winter" caused by the increased atmospheric opacity from the air-borne debris and dust.

Thermonuclear war is another persistent fear that did abate for a while after the end of the cold war between the United States and the then Soviet Union. However, recent events, including threats of a nuclear strike from Russian president Vladimir Putin, have brought public attention back to this terrifying possibility. Indeed, the conflagration could start at any time, whether intentionally or through some accident.

Some people even fear an alien invasion like H.G. Wells' *War of the Worlds*. Others don't fear the complete destruction of the planet or the human race, but just see a coming economic collapse that will forever destroy their ways of life, and send us back into the dark ages.

Some of these dangers are problems of faith rather than fact, some are rabidly paranoid fantasies, and some, while certainly possible, are not terribly likely in our time. Nonetheless, some of them could suddenly become horrifyingly real and wipe us out while the television cameras roll. But fortunately, among these more likely mass disasters might be some we could deal with, if only we could function as one people in worldwide unity.

If mankind could coordinate the disparate scientific and medical capabilities of all the advanced nations, the world could likely minimize the devastation of a pandemic. If there was an international nuclear force combining the arsenals of the US, Russia and China with all other nuclear states working together, we might be able to destroy or divert an incoming asteroid, or even a comet, with a massive, mutually-launched barrage of carefully targeted nuclear weapons. And most importantly, if that worldwide military institution did indeed control all nuclear weapons and had the power to end war as a means of dispute resolution, nuclear annihilation would become, if not impossible, pretty much a nightmare of the past.

Even the fear of economic disaster could be eliminated by the existence of effective and well-intentioned worldwide financial institutions that had the power to ensure stable and available means of exchange. Since there is plenty of food, clothing and other necessities in the world, or if production was ramped up until there was, were there an economic system that could distribute those things equitably, nobody would have to live without them. But this should not be done through a socialistic or communist model, however a very wise and powerful worldwide organization could efficiently distribute goods to those in need, while protecting the more prosperous peoples' wealth, whether hard-earned or fairly-inherited.

Yet, in spite of the advantages of a world-wide government, many people fear it as a potential tyranny from which there would be no escape. These people prefer to live as they have for their whole lives, protected by their national governments, most of which do attempt to meet the needs of their populations.

People also point out how powerless and ineffective the United Nations has been, and how a world government, if democratic, would be controlled by populous third world nations who would see it as a tool for redistribution of wealth on a national scale. Why, they ask, should powerful nations submit themselves to the popular will of nations who would vote to strip them of their wealth, power and influence? Worse yet, those numerous third-world nations might also lack the economic and political skills to use those assets to institute productive policies.

Clearly, a purely democratic world government would not work under current conditions, or under any conditions likely to transpire in the near term. And the alternative of a tyrannical world government that is ruled by the unchecked dictates of the wealthy and powerful is equally undesirable. What is needed is a hybrid structure that does not adhere to any preconceived political system, but is designed strictly to work, that is functioning to meet the economic and political needs of the world. The challenge is to overcome the nationalistic objections from the populations, and especially the elites, of the powerful nations.

One thing is certain, new international institutions could not be revolutionary in nature. They must not overturn the existing nexuses that might be called the-powers-that-be. People of wealth and power generally didn't get what they have by way of accident, they have skill sets that have been developed over lives of achievement or over generations of hereditary position and leadership. There are few people within the middle or lower classes who have the chops to exercise world leadership. The problem is that these wealthy, powerful people have been working behind the scenes for generations as they no doubt feel that they must, to maintain an acceptable world order, but even more important to them, to safeguarding their own wealth and power. In most countries, elected officials essentially do their bidding while using their offices to influence mass acceptance of the necessary policies secretly handed down to presidents, premiers and prime ministers from the true powers-that-be above.

The corollary here is that there already is a world government, but it functions via an unstable system of competing factions, with no transparency whatsoever. This secret world government implements their own agendas or activities, completely unaccountable to the great masses of people who are subject to their wills, and are often decimated by their power struggles.

Another problem is that while working behind the scenes, the powers-that-be feel the need to preserve their anonymity and opacity, even to the point of secrecy. A great deal of their effort must be directed toward simply preserving their power, because they do not have deep-seated confidence that their leadership would be accepted by the public masses if revealed. This actually limits their ability to work in the public interest, as they must always take into account the need to act in self interest to preserve their secret status and power.

What is required is for the world to accept that these great behind-the-scenes powers, some individuals, some social classes, some formal and informal groupings, who do study and develop policies, be recognized, legitimized and empowered to transparently exercise leadership in the public eye and in the public interest.

But these people who already have stewardship of the world, for all their virtues, are still human and capable of abusing their powers. If there were to be a world government, there would need to be a world constitution with the sort of checks and balances that make the American and British systems some of the more workable on the planet. There would have to be voices for those that now have no say in their own fates. There would have to be sufficient institutionalized power to enable the wealthy to preserve their wealth or they would never accept the system. In short, the system must accept the status quo or the status quo would never accept the system. There would have to be a strong central leader that was positioned to be above the need for any personal gain and who thus could serve in the broadest public interest.

What about the United Nations, isn't that an effort to create just such institutions with the Security Council protecting the prerogatives of the powerful and the general assembly giving voice to all? In those limited ways, the UN did get it right. But the UN could be compared to the first effort to unite the 13 states in America after independence from Britain. The Articles of Confederation were a complete failure for many of the same reasons that the United Nations is ineffective today – in particular a lack of central authority. In the case of the Articles, this was because the 13 states each envisioned themselves as nations unto themselves. Hence, they were loathe to turn over any important elements of their "national" sovereignty to a central authority, and the national government was left with few powers and no revenues.

Nations such as America, Russia, China, Japan, Britain, Germany, France, India, Brazil and a few others with great wealth and power must make a decision, however difficult, to cede some of their sovereign powers to a world authority. While anathema to many, upon deeper reflection, who would not prefer this outcome to thermonuclear war? However, it is important that the vital interests of all the great nations be addressed and preserved, or they will impede any effort to develop the new institutions and policies that the world and all its nations need to survive, develop and prosper.

A workable bicameral structure might have a Senate or upper house composed of everybody with a certain level of existing wealth, power and prestige. In other words, all the people who currently rule the planet in secrecy. This might include the world's multi-billionaires and its most powerful bankers, central or otherwise. It should include major stockholders, CEOs and presidents of the large national and multinational corporations. It would certainly include media moguls and powerful media spokespersons. It must above all include the time-tested titled nobility and sitting royal families of the world, creating recognition of their long-standing, if subtle, power and obvious public importance, not to mention their unique understanding of leadership and power in a long-term context.

This world senate would give these powerful people a viable means of publically exercising the power they currently exercise secretly. Their seats in the Senate would be guaranteed for life, much as are those of the members of the House of Lords in Great Britain.

Without the need to perform their self-serving maneuvers and machinations in private, these powerful people could bring their extraordinary abilities into the light, serving the public interests with the assurance that their power and prerogatives would be preserved and institutionalized. But if this legislature would be bicameral, what about the lower house?

It would be the top elected officials of all nations, but therein is a problem. Perhaps since the dawn of democracy, but certainly in the way that democracy has ultimately flowered, elected officials have relied on campaign funds to compete successfully in their elections. This has, to a greater or lesser extent, made them beholden to those with the financial resources to thus assist them. Conversely, the wealthy and powerful have felt it important to ensure the election of individuals whose points of view are acceptable to them – no raving populists, please.

But, with their positions of power acknowledged and institutionalized in the world senate, these powerful people could let the forces of democracy function as many imagine they already do. So, there would finally have to be a system that produces elected leadership who do not necessarily have to be acceptable to the wealthy. If so, they could strongly advocate for the interests of those who are not members of the elite. Then, the national governments could advance the grass roots body politics of these nations, and the general interests of their populations. All candidates would receive equal campaign stipends from their national governments, and nothing else, so there would be no influence peddling to gain campaign funds. Thus, a president would no longer be dancing to the tune of his or her wealthy and powerful backers, and could at last truly represent and serve the needs of the electorates who vote them in. These elected national leaders, in addition to their executive duties within their national regions, would hold seats in the lower house of the World Congress, controlling voting power proportional to an index reflecting their nations' populations, but also their gross domestic products, and all other important measures of national power and influence. All these representatives would hold their seats in the lower house for as long as they hold their national offices, with their seats passing on to whoever replaces them.

Underpinning this legislative structure would be a World Constitution specifying this or a similar realistic approach to bringing the real power elite of the world into a position of legitimate governance, but also into a great deal more transparency and accountability. The World Constitution would also create executive and judicial branches to institute checks and balances. The executive, or head of state, would be chosen by a two-thirds majority vote within the upper house only, since these people are the real powers-that-be and rulers of the world. To be effective, the executive would have to be completely acceptable to them. The world cannot afford push-pull governance such as has ravaged the United States at times. Members of the judicial branch, in this case a World Supreme Court, would be selected by the upper house, but would have to be ratified by the lower house. Lower courts would exist only as organs of the various national governments. Each national government would be responsible for the civil and criminal laws and courts within their own borders.

There would be no restrictions on trade, such as tarifs, instituted by the national governments, but the World Government would have the duty to regulate trade, when necessary, to ensure the economic stability of each nation state. To make a purely free trade system more acceptable to the developed nations' work forces, there would have to be a worldwide minimum wage system so companies could not use ultra-low wage third world workers to strip workers in the developed world of their jobs. The worldwide minimum wage would be determined on a sliding scale to enable some fair and modest degree of advantage to developing populations to offset the additional risk of using less skilled workers.

The economic system would be very close to *laissez faire* capitalism, but there would be a rigorous anti-trust unit within the World Judiciary Branch to prevent unfair combinations or monopolies from stifling beneficial competition. Any corporate entities that do achieve monopoly status likely did so by out-performing their competition, so they will not be sanctioned or punished for their achievement, rather the leading executives will be inducted into the upper legislative house, if not already there, in recognition of their having achieved dominance of their industry. Nonetheless, the monopolistic company will be horizontally divided into a new set of competitors and, if necessary, would also be divided vertically so that the resulting entities do not also unfairly compete with rival suppliers, distributors and transportation companies.

There would also be readily available government funding for promising new enterprises, particularly advanced technologies that have the potential to increase the standard of living and/or quality of life worldwide or in any major area. Funding would still be available directly from the world's private banks as now, but also from a world financial authority based on a special panel's assessment of the merit of the project and the financial responsibility of the applicant. These new public funds would be made available to both start-up enterprises and existing companies, large and small.

The economic objectives of the world government will be to raise the standard of living of those whose lives and means are below average, but not at the expense of reducing the means of the more prosperous citizens of the world. They should not be punished for their economic achievements and success, whether measured on any scale from the individual to the national. Industries deemed essential for the welfare of the world's people that are for any reason unable to self-sustain financially, will be subsidized, not as a reward for an inadequate performance, which in any event may be due to factors beyond anyone's control, but in service of the general good.

A policy's effect on the general good will be the primary yardstick used to determine the shape and force of that policy. For example, as of the time of this writing, several nations' inability to service their national debts, potentially including even the United States, are threatening to destroy the entire world's economy. Imagine the effect of the United States defaulting on its debt. Under a world government, any regions that cannot achieve self-sufficiency will be assisted in meeting their obligations, but more importantly in growing their economies. Defaults will be eliminated so creditors and bond holders will always be paid, however the financial power will not be able to use the weakness or lack of creditworthiness of the debtor as a reason to charge higher interest rates and further weaken them. Each case will be assessed by a panel of economic and financial experts, and policies will be implemented that foster the common good rather than further punishing and crippling a nation or corporation already in economic pain. In a world where there is no default, interest rates for nation states and other political or economic entities that need or receive private funding will be lower since there is virtually no risk.

Political problems will be handled with decisive pragmatism and with the goal of a win-win outcome for all parties. For example, one of the most dangerous problems facing the world right now is the situation between the Israeli state and Palestinian people. As most know, the problem arose when the post-Holocaust remainder of the Jewish people won the right to return, after two millennia, to their ancestral homeland. Granted, this was implemented through the power of interested third party nations who had their own agendas regarding the post-World War II disposition of the important oil-rich region. But it seemed to many a historical necessity that Western Civilization should give the Jewish people the security of their own nation state, and it is a historical reality that the state of Israel now exists again.

However, for two millennia the Jewish people did not live in what has been called Palestine since the Roman Empire expelled the Jews after a couple of failed revolts. For those two thousand years, this was the homeland of the Palestinians. Since Israel was recreated and the Palestinians were stripped of their nation, they have sought a right to return to their former homes and businesses in what is now Israel. Most international experts who've evaluated this most difficult situation believe the answer is what's called a two-state solution. But where would the new Palestinian state be? The West Bank of the Jordan River is what has been suggested, but Israel will never give that up because losing it would leave a geographically indefensible nation. But there has been no better answer to the two-state solution. Meanwhile, there have been several wars and there is no end in sight, with the potential for an Armageddon extinction event war, after all that is a place name in this region and a possible and likely flash point for a third world war.

The Palestinians are well-educated and productive people and could be exemplary citizens of the world, if they were not bedeviled by decades of life in refugee camps, the reality of the deprivation of their ancestral homeland, and the righteous feelings of injustice that have stirred them to acts of violence and terror.

Here is a problem that is hard to solve without a world government, but very easy to solve with one in place. The involved parties, that is the Israelis and other prosperous Jewish people throughout the world, on the one hand, and the Arab, Iranian and other Muslim people, awash in oil wealth on the other hand, with the financial and political support of the world government – that is to say the rest of the world's peoples – will create a new nation state for the Palestinian people that will fully meet their aspirations and needs.

It will not be the same real estate they once occupied, but it will be adjacent and contiguous to some of their current area, the Gaza Strip. It will extend south and west from the Gaza Strip into Egypt's Sinai desert along Egypt's border with Israel, but will not include Egypt's existing oil-producing regions or coastal areas. Preferably this re-bordering will result from a negotiated settlement with Egypt, no doubt at a very high price, but otherwise Egypt will be compelled to accept an extremely high and beyond-fair price for the cession of a portion of their national land.

This new Palestinian state will be developed from what is now relatively unoccupied desert. It will then be, using the world's financial and technological resources, developed into a garden state. This will no doubt require plenty of water from massive desalinization plants sufficient to turn the previously parched deserts into prime farmland. It will also be equipped with an infrastructure that will enable a solid economic and industrial base. Whatever the cost of this solution, it will pale in comparison to the "costs" of World War III!

The many other problems that plague the world's peoples will also be addressed by the World Government with equal pragmatism. Undeveloped nations will receive such resources as it takes to raise their standards of living to a level enabling healthy conditions, the opportunity for all to receive educations, and with sufficient infrastructure to create real economic opportunity. No nation will have its natural resources plundered going forward without benefit accruing to that nation's people, but no corporations who have invested to develop those resources will be deprived of the return on their investment as might occur now in a hostile nationalization.

All the world's citizens will be protected from exploitation by a worldwide minimum wage system that is linked to regional costs of living and the various productivity levels that exist in a given population. This minimum wage system will not only protect the workers in the less developed nations, but will also protect the workers in the more developed nations by reducing the temptation in corporate boardrooms to increase profits by outsourcing their labor forces to areas where workers are virtual slaves. If the right system can be instituted, it should eventually be very close to self-regulating and will gradually elevate low-wage workers into enough prosperity so that they will become an economic engine. Increasing these workers' levels of pay, and thus consumption, will fuel creation of more jobs at home and elsewhere. These workers will not only create more demand, but will also be creating more supply, resulting in a net gain in worldwide economic activity.

But these are just examples of what might be achieved if the world actually created an institution that can set and perhaps achieve the objectives necessary for a free, prosperous and safe world, a world where parents can raise their children without so much fear, and where children can grow and thrive in a truly civilized environment that gives them hope, security and opportunity.

Would such a world government be desirable? Many don't think so, and will fight to preserve national prerogatives and power. But imagine for a moment if the United States was not united but just a few dozen little nations, each state fully independent and sovereign, sometimes cooperating, but always competing and on occasion fighting. Is it so horrible that an overarching power was created to regulate their interactions and coordinate their policies? Why would it not eventually accrue at least the same benefits to have the world's nations thus working together for the common good, under the authority of reliable and well-meaning institutional entities? At any rate, a solution like this is certainly more desirable than economic collapse and/or worldwide thermonuclear destruction.

For this to happen, the well-meaning and patriotic citizens of the various nation states should turn their attention from the idea of preventing the creation of a World Government, really a hopeless task when an informal, opaque and unaccountable world order already exists, to the task of instituting one that truly meets the needs of the world and its people. We now have a World Government that is secretive and unregulated, what we need is a World Constitution, truly establishing and empowering the Earth's rulers to stop being concerned about protecting or growing their own power, and freeing them to work on everyone's behalf. Thus, freed from the demands of self-preservation, they can bring their powers and skills to the tasks of ending starvation and poverty while banning warfare as an institution.

But if the upper and lower houses were duly constituted, and all the world's most powerful people became the world's first effective legislative branch, what would be the nature of the executive branch? And who could radiate the power and prestige needed to command the world's respect, while also embodying the human and spiritual qualities needed to steer this massive new ship of state? This individual must perform executive duties with justice, firmness, kindness, compassion and a genuine love of humanity. This person must have the strength of breeding and character to perform executive duties with an iron hand when necessary, only with the goal of bringing peace, grace and mercy to the lives of all the world's peoples.

On the world's stage today, there could only be one individual who might have all these properties, and more. That person is William, His Royal Highness Prince of Wales. Here is an example of humanity at its very best, a man who we can look up to, but at the same time we can look across at as one of us, his warmth and humanity self-evident to all.

So here is our brave new world, the powers-that-be, whether those powers derive from station, birth or achievement, given formal status as members of the upper legislative house, freed of the need to protect position and power and finally able to exercise their talents for the betterment of the world. Working with them to bring a greater awareness of the peoples of the world needs. At times, checking and balancing the upper house, would be a lower house composed of the highest elected officials of all the nation states. They would wield voting power reflective of their nations' populations, but also adjusted to acknowledge other measures of national importance to include gross domestic product and their military contribution to the world's instruments of preserving order. These legislative bodies must be formed and configured to reflect, not alter, the realities of world power or they will be artificial and ultimately meaningless. They must also carry within their structures a responsive flexibility enabling periodic adaption to changing realities or conditions.

And embodying, symbolizing and bringing genuine leadership to this new worldwide organization, and ruling within the powers established for his position by the new World Constitution, would be William, His Royal Highness Prince of Wales. We can only pray that worthy successors will arise when he wishes to step down and pass the mantle to another.

These policies are this writer's prayers: a world where all nations, religions and classes honor and appreciate each other, while staying true to their own customs and beliefs; a world where scientific truth is seen as the manifestation of the Divine truth that it is; and a world that has finally learned to govern itself for the common betterment of all mankind. Amen.

NOTES

[1] Muktananda, Swami, *I Have Become Alive, Secrets of the Inner Journey*, 2nd Edition (South Fallsburg, NY, Syda Foundation, 1985) p.139

[2] Davies, Paul, *The Mind of God: The Scientific Basis for a Rational World*, (New York, NY Simon & Schuster Paperbacks, 1992) p.16

[3]CERN, Dark matter: Invisible dark matter makes up most of the universe…https://home.cern/science/physics/dark-matter#:~:text=Dark%20matter%20seems%20to%20outweigh,about%2027%25%20of%20the%20universe, Accessed March 6, 2024

[4]Susskind, Leonard, *The Black Hole War, My Battle with Steven Hawking to Make the World Safe for Quantum Mechanics* (New York, NY, Little, Brown Company, 2008) p.302

[5]Davies, Paul, *The Mind of God: The Scientific Basis for a Rational World,* (New York, NY, Simon & Schuster Paperbacks, 1992) p.158

BIBLIOGRAPHY

Davies, Paul, *The Cosmic Blueprint: New Discoveries in Nature's Creative Abilities to Order the Universe*. Philadelphia, PA and London, England: The Templeton Foundation Press, 2004.

Goswami, Amit, Ph.D. with Richard Reed and Maggie Goswami, *The Self-Aware Universe: How Consciousness Creates the Physical World.* New York, NY: Jeremy P. Tarcher/Putnam, a member of Penguin Putnam, Inc. 1995.

Muktananda, Swami. *I Have Become Alive, Secrets of the Inner Journey*, 2nd Edition. South Fallsburg, NY: Syda Foundation, 1985.

Lazlo, Ervin, *Science and the Akashic Field: An Integral Theory of Everything*. Rochester, VT: Inner Traditions, 2007.

Pakula, Dennis, *New Story, New God: A Reconsidering of the Relationship Between Scientific Theory and God Talk.* Titusville, FL, Four Seasons Publishers, 1999.

Sheldrake, Riupert, *A New Science of Life: The Hypothesis of Formative Causation*: Los Angeles, CA, J.P. Tarcher, 1981

Susskind, Leonard. *The Black Hole War, My Battle with Steven Hawking to Make the World Safe for Quantum Mechanics*. New York, NY Little, Brown Company, 2008

Talbot, Michael. *The Holographic Universe the Revolutionary Theory of Reality*: New York, NY, HarperCollins Publishers, 2011

von Kreisler, Kristin. *The Compassion of Animals, The True Stories of Animal Courage and Kindness*: Boston, MA, G K Hall & Co. 1998

INDEX

abominations, 152
Absolute, 158, 176-179
acceptance, 98, 144, 150, 151, 160, 176, 178, 179, 189
Aesculapius, 105
Akashic Record, 37, 38, 39, 50, 60
alchemy, 94
Alexander the Great, 98
alien invasion, 186
Allah, 91, 104, 147, 158
America, 2, 191
amino acids, 24, 116, 130
amoebas, 94, 95, 114, 119, 133
amphibians, 116
anti-Semitism, 172
Arjuna, 84, 85
Armageddon, 153, 185
Aspect, Alain, 4, 30, 32
asteroid, 185, 187
awareness, 43, 44, 46, 47, 49, 180, 201
bacteria, 94, 95, 112, 113, 119
Baptists, 146, 164
basketball players, 45
Bhagavad Gita, 84, 174
Bible, 5, 24, 37, 68, 78, 80, 103, 106, 174
Big Bang, 8-11, 13-15, 17, 24-28, 134, 141, 183, 184
birds, 47, 114, 119-122, 124
black hole, 18, 19, 57, 58, 59, 181
Bohm, David, 4, 30, 35, 37, 58
bonobo chimpanzees, 99
Book of Revelation, 103
Brazil, 191
Britain, 190, 191
Buddhism, 90, 158, 176-179
Cabalistic Judaism, 173
Caduceus of Mercury, 105
caldera, 186
California Literary Review, 59
Catholics, 146, 164, 169
cause and effect, 57, 176, 178
cellular division, 94, 96, 111, 116, 117
centers of consciousness, 69, 149
CERN, 51, 52, 53
chakra, 4, 68, 72-78, 80-89, 91-94, 96-98, 100, 101, 105, 107-109, 116-120, 122-131, 162, 163
China, 176, 187, 191
Christianity, 64, 84, 103, 131, 155, 156, 158, 161, 163-167, 170, 173, 175
church, 134, 146, 155, 171
Churchill, Winston, 98
cold-blooded, 114
comet, 185
compassion, 39, 77-80, 81, 84-86, 90, 93, 124-126, 140, 200
consciousness, 11-14, 16, 17, 19, 21, 22, 24, 26-29, 37, 44, 49, 50, 58, 59, 60-62, 67-69, 71, 72, 74, 81-83, 87-89, 90, 93, 94, 96, 103-105, 107-109, 115, 130-132, 137-142, 148, 149, 160, 162, 163, 175, 176, 182
cosmological constant, 22
Council of Nicaea, 84, 162, 165
counter culture, 155
creation, 6, 8, 10-15, 17, 24-26, 28, 29, 68, 84, 93, 103, 104, 110, 111, 116, 118, 119, 123, 126, 128-133, 135, 137, 138, 144, 146, 154, 155, 163, 184, 199, 200
Creationists, 110
Creator, 7, 8, 11, 29, 31, 89, 91, 113, 144, 147, 151-153, 173, 184
crown of creation, 128
cutting, 3, 50, 72, 95, 101
Dark Energy, 16, 17, 22, 23, 26, 27, 29, 52, 53, 113, 115, 131, 133, 184
dark matter, 22, 23, 51-54, 203
Darwinian evolution, 110, 112, 113, 118
Darwinists, 112

Davies, Paul, 3, 4, 41, 180, 203, 204
death, 2, 18, 19, 50, 57, 59-65, 70, 76, 85, 89, 94-96, 100, 134, 136, 137, 156, 165, 167, 169, 178
Declaration on Animal Consciousness, 88
déjà vu, 40
depopulation, 186
determinism, 57, 59
devil, 112, 147
dinosaurs, 111, 115, 119, 121, 185
DNA, 106, 117, 129, 181, 184
double helix, 106-108, 130, 184
$E = mc^2$, 21
Egyptian Pharaohs, 106
Einstein, Albert, 14, 21, 27, 32, 33, 42
empathy, 39, 43, 48, 77, 81, 124, 125
enlightenment, 107
Enlightenment, 177
entangled particles, 33, 36
entangled photons, 32, 33, 35
entanglement, 1, 41-44, 46, 47, 49
entropy, 111, 113, 115, 129
esoteric knowledge, 175
evolution, 2, 13, 14, 25, 73, 110-115, 118, 119, 123-130, 182
evolutionary theory, 111
executive branch, 200
exodus, 174
extra-sensory perception, 32
Fermilab, 36, 37, 52
fish, 47, 111, 114, 116, 120, 122
fossil record, 13, 112, 114, 115, 119
France, 166, 172, 191
Freemasonry, 94
Freud, Sigmund, 95
Genesis, 24, 25, 80, 110, 111, 129, 132, 174
genetic engineering, 129
genitals, 76, 116, 117
genocide, 172
Germany, 191
God, 2, 1, 2, 4-9, 11-17, 19, 24-29, 37, 41, 57, 64, 66, 68, 71, 80, 83-85, 88-94, 98, 106, 107, 109, 110, 112, 113, 115-121, 123, 126, 128-167, 169-185, 203, 204
Gomorrah, 174
gradualism, 114
Great Cycle of Creation, 14-17, 28, 88, 107
guided evolution, 113, 115, 129
hadiths, 170
Hamlet's soliloquy, 62
hara, 71, 72
harakiri, 72
heart, 3, 67, 69-71, 73, 74, 97, 116, 139, 149, 164
Heaven's Gate, 143
hedonism, 155
Herophilus, 87
heterosexuality, 94, 97
Hindu, 67, 80, 84, 96, 105, 106, 175, 176, 184
Hinduism, 37, 66, 158, 173-175
Hitler, Adolph, 73, 85, 109, 141
Holocaust, 85, 139, 140, 172, 196
hologram, 31, 34-39, 46, 54-56, 60-64
holographic substrate, 41, 54, 55
holographic universe, 1, 7, 34, 36-38, 49, 50, 164
Homo heidelbergensis, 127
Homo sapiens, 82, 85, 112, 126, 130
homosexuality, 97, 98
Hooft, Gerard 't, 4, 30, 35
Hopis, 67
hunting and feeding behaviors, 125
hurricanes, 138
India, 38, 176, 191
inquisition, 161
instinctive behavior, 121, 124
intelligent design, 2, 111, 112
Internet, 185
interrupted equilibria, 114, 115, 128
intuition, 49
Islam, 76, 104, 147, 158, 166-168, 170, 171
Japan, 71, 172, 176
Jehovah's Witnesses, 146

Jesus, 64, 83, 84, 131, 148, 162-164, 166, 173
jihad, 161, 168
Jihadist, 143
Judaism, 103, 148, 158, 170, 171, 173
Judeo-Christians, 15
Kabbalah, 103
karma, 176
Kersten, Felix,139
Krishna, 85
Kundalini, 106, 130, 184
laissez faire, 194
László, Erwin, 3, 25, 37, 60, 125
laws of thermodynamics, 110, 112, 113
Lennon, John, 98
Lincoln, Abraham, 98
lounge lizard, 117
love, 1, 20, 29, 39, 43, 48, 64, 67, 69, 70, 71, 74, 77-79, 84, 86, 90, 93, 108, 120-123, 126, 137, 138, 140, 156, 165, 178, 200
lower house, 192, 193, 201
Macedonians, 98
mammals, 93, 112, 114, 115, 119, 120-124, 126
martyrs, 90, 165
masochism, 95, 96, 100
Matthew 6:22, 83
Mayans, 67
Mecca, 104
Middle East, 168
Milky Way, 132
minimum wage, 194, 198
missionary, 152, 161
modern man, 112, 114, 129
Mohammed, 166, 167, 169, 170
monotheism, 170, 171, 174
Moses, 106, 107, 163, 173, 181
mosque, 171
Muktananda, Swami, 11, 203, 204
multi-cellular organisms, 111
nature, 2, 14, 31, 33, 48, 51, 58, 80, 85, 93, 96, 111, 115, 121, 138, 159, 173, 177-180, 188, 200
Nazis, 139, 140
Nbiru, 185
Neanderthal, 126
Neanderthals, 128
Nirvana, 177
Nobel Prize, 35
non-local connection, 44, 46, 47
North America, 186
Nostradamus, 38
nuclear weapons, 154, 187
nucleotides, 24, 116
number seven, 103, 104
Old Testament, 106
ornithologists, 124
pandemic, 186, 187
Pandora, 91, 100, 101
Pandora's Box, 100, 101
parasympathetic system, 87
particle accelerators, 160, 173
penance, 172
Penrose, Sir Roger, 26
People's Temple, 143
philosopher's stone, 94
pineal gland, 86, 87
Planck's constant, 36
Plato, 38
pogroms, 172
point of the sword, 167
Pope, 9, 11, 165, 169
populists, 192
premiers, 189
Presbyterians, 146
proselytizing, 161
Protestant reformation, 166
Protestants, 164
quantum entanglement, 1, 7, 41, 44, 45, 48, 49, 166
Quetzalcoatl, 106
Quintessence, 16, 22, 29, 184
rapture, 185
realpolitik, 72
reptiles, 75, 111, 114, 116, 119, 121-123
righteousness, 160, 170, 171
rite of passage, 91, 144-147, 151, 158-160, 163, 164, 166, 168, 170, 171, 173, 176, 181

Roman, 165, 172
Russia, 187, 191
sacral plexus, 74
sacral-coccygeal ganglia, 91, 92
sadism, 95, 96, 100
Sanskrit, 4, 106, 149
science, 1, 2, 4, 7, 17, 18, 22, 29, 31-33, 38, 43, 64, 80, 86, 111, 112, 115, 116, 118, 156, 159, 160, 173, 180-184, 203
Scrooge, Ebenezer, 108
sea turtle, 120
secular humanism, 5, 155
serpent energy, 106
Seventh Day Adventists, 146, 164
sexual desire, 74
sexual reproduction, 115, 116, 118
sharia, 76, 168
Shiites, 168-170
sin, 73, 108, 109, 175, 177
Sodom, 174
solar plexus, 71-73, 97, 116, 119
solar system, 52, 185
Spartans, 98
spawning, 122, 168
speaking in tongues, 147
speed of light, 32, 33
Sri Lanka, 176
Staff of Aesculapius, 105
status quo, 98, 190
submission, 99, 147, 166, 169, 170
Sunnis, 168, 170
Supreme Being, 158, 176
Susskind, Leonard, 3, 4, 18, 30, 31, 34, 35, 54, 57-59, 204
sympathy, 43, 77
synagogue, 171
Talbot, Michael, 31, 39
Ten Commandments, 75, 165, 171
tennis players, 45
Thanatos, 94, 95
The Big Crunch, 16, 52, 53, 183
the Divine, 5, 68, 144, 151, 152, 163, 177, 181
The Great Spirit, 177
the Word, 80, 83
Theravada, 176
thermonuclear war, 191
Thorn, Charles, 4, 30, 35
tolerance, 150, 151
tornados, 138
transcendence, 160, 176, 179
Transcendence, 177
transmutation, 93, 108
trigeminal ganglion, 87
true believer, 5, 146
tsunamis, 138
turbans, 88
unicellular organisms, 112
United Nations, 188, 190
United States, 2, 125, 172, 193, 195, 199
Upanishads, 174
Vedas, 174
vertebrates, 116
War of the Worlds, 186
warm-blooded, 114, 120
wave function, 57
Wells, H.G., 186
World Congress, 193
World Constitution, 193, 200
world government, 188, 189, 195, 197, 199, 200
World Judiciary Branch, 194
World Supreme Court, 193
worldwide minimum wage, 194
yarmulke, 88
ye of little faith, 148
Yellowstone, 186
Yeshua, 162
yoga, 83, 90, 107, 175
zero-sum theory, 10
Zeus, 105

Made in the USA
Columbia, SC
12 August 2024

39887054R00131